ADHD Workbook for Women

Improve Focus, Get Organized, Avoid Emotional Spending, and Overcome Other ADHD Challenges

Tracy Neel

© Copyright 2023 – Tracy Neel - All rights reserved

The content within this book may not be reproduced, duplicated, or transmitted without direct written permission from the author or the publisher.

Under no circumstances will any blame or legal responsibility be held against the publisher, or author, for any damages, reparation, or monetary loss due to the information contained within this book, either directly or indirectly.

Legal Notice

This book is copyright protected. This book is only for personal use. You cannot amend, distribute, sell, use, quote, or paraphrase any part, or the content within this book, without the consent of the author-publisher.

Disclaimer Notice

Please note that the information contained within this document is for educational and entertainment purposes only. All effort has been executed to present accurate, up-to-date, and reliable, complete information. No warranties of any kind are declared or implied. Readers acknowledge that the author is not engaging in the rendering of legal, financial, medical, or professional advice.

TABLE OF CONTENTS

INTRODUCTION 6

CHAPTER 1: UNDERSTANDING ADHD 10

    Different Types of ADHD 12

    Causes of ADHD 14

    Co-existing Conditions With ADHD 15

    ADHD in Women – The Challenge 18

    Diagnosing ADHD 23

    Treatment 26

CHAPTER 2: COPING WITH ADHD 29

    Mindfulness and Self-Awareness 29

    Overcoming Indecisiveness 32

    Finding the Degree of Uncertainty 34

    Time Management 38

    Managing Stress Through Relaxation 47

    Using Exercise to Help Manage Your ADHD Better 50

Chapter 3: IMPROVING RELATIONSHIPS 54

    Romantic Relationships 54

    Maintaining Healthy Relationships With Family and Friends 57

    Building Supportive Networks 59

CHAPTER 4: MANAGING DAILY LIFE WITH ADHD 63

    Home Organization and Management 63

    Emotional Spending 70

Coping With ADHD-Related Challenges in Education and Career 73

CHAPTER 5: BUILDING RESILIENCE 76

Resilience – Its Role in ADHD 76

Developing a Growth Mindset and Positive Self-Talk 77

Embracing Your Strengths and Talents 78

Realistic Goal-Setting With ADHD 81

Helping Other Women With ADHD 86

CHAPTER 6: BALANCING LIFE AND ADHD 88

Finding Balance and Managing Burnout 88

Setting Boundaries and Taking Care of Oneself 91

Finding New Interests to Improve Life Satisfaction 92

CHAPTER 7: OVERCOMING PROCRASTINATION AND PERFECTIONISM 95

Procrastination and Perfectionism – Understanding Their Role in ADHD 96

Developing a Growth Mindset and Letting Go of Perfectionism 97

Practical Strategies for Overcoming Procrastination 99

CHAPTER 8: NAVIGATING THE WORKPLACE WITH ADHD 102

Understanding the Impact of ADHD on Career Success 102

Navigating Accommodations in the Workplace With ADHD 104

Building Self-Advocacy Skills and Seeking Support at Work 106

CHAPTER 9: MANAGING RELATIONSHIPS AND SEXUALITY WITH ADHD 112

How Does Your ADHD Impact Your Intimate Relationship? 112

Sexual Health and ADHD 113

CHAPTER 10: EXECUTIVE FUNCTIONING AND ADHD 116

Strategies for Improving Executive Functioning 118

CHAPTER 11: STRESS MANAGEMENT AND EMOTIONAL REGULATION 128

Stress and ADHD 128

Managing Stress With ADHD 129

Emotional Dysregulation and ADHD 131

Emotional Regulation in Men Versus Women With ADHD 132

Strategies to Help Regulate Emotions 133

Regulating Your Emotions and Reducing Negative Thoughts With ADHD 143

CHAPTER 12: MANAGING ATTENTION AND FOCUS 145

Strategies to Improve Focus and Attention 146

Tips to Help Reduce Distractions 149

Techniques to Help You Stay on Task 150

CHAPTER 13: BUILDING HEALTHY HABITS AND ROUTINES 154

Tips for Creating and Maintaining Healthy Habits 155

Creating an ADHD-Friendly Morning Routine 156

Creating an ADHD-Friendly Evening Routine 157

Designing a Personalized Daily Routine 158

CHAPTER 14: PROFESSIONAL HELP AND SUPPORT 163

Finding the Right Treatment That Works for You 163

Importance of Seeking Professional Help 165

Reach Out a Helping Hand 167

CONCLUSION 168

ABOUT THE AUTHOR 170

INTRODUCTION

Attention deficit hyperactivity disorder, widely-known as ADHD, is one of the most common neurodevelopmental disorders. It is usually diagnosed in children but persists in adulthood as well.

You may ask yourself, "What if I was not diagnosed as a child?" If you are reading this book, you are probably one of the many misdiagnosed women with ADHD. There has been an increase in the diagnoses of female adult ADHD and the number of female patients seeking help for their problems. Why? Because throughout their lives, they have been told they suffer from everything *except* ADHD.

The majority of newly diagnosed women with adult ADHD feel relieved since they can now understand their issues, which usually differ from the conventional "male" version. Even the manual used for diagnosing mental health disorders including ADHD has most of its research based on male ADHD. Women are disregarded and less likely to be referred for mental health services as a result of the stereotypes associated with ADHD. As you read this you realize you know this far too well.

It is important to keep in mind that ADHD is not gender specific. A lot of people associate ADHD with mischievous, unruly schoolboys who would bounce off the walls. Its symptoms are equally prevalent in both boys and girls. There is a significant gender discrepancy in the diagnosis rate, with males roughly three times more likely than girls to receive an ADHD diagnosis.

Women's ADHD presents differently. As a result, many young women experience a sense of confusion. Their problems are occasionally misdiagnosed as "hormonal" or "anxiety" issues. Sometimes, the symptoms of ADHD are linked to personality traits like being "the talkative ones" and being more sociable. As women are expected to be more organized, society becomes less tolerant of them when they slip up. Because of this when women seek professional help, they tend to under-report their symptoms, and when they do, their hormonal changes are often never taken into consideration in the assessment.

You might be wondering how hormonal changes could affect your ADHD. Well, you go through puberty, menstruation, pregnancy, and menopause; all stages of life that fluctuate your hormone levels. The more internalizing effects of ADHD, cause women to self-diagnose, self-medicate, engage in risky sexual behavior, and risk suffering from chronic pain, amongst many others.

This workbook is going to help you find yourself in this world and help you thrive with your valuable skills; those you have had all your life but never knew how to put into practice. You struggled to keep your desk organized, and your apartment clean. You struggled with attending social events and not feeling anxious. You have put off joining a fitness class or enrolling at a new gym because it gives you anxiety. You have struggled with maintaining healthy eating habits, being consistent with your daily routine, and overall living in distress. Have you noticed how I am outlining these things as if they happened in the past, and are no longer occurring now? That is because this is going to be you from now on. You are going to learn some crucial skills that you should have known all along, but no one passed on this knowledge to you.

From understanding ADHD, its symptoms, and all that comes with it, to actual realistic approaches that will change your life for the better, this workbook has everything you need to know. I am not going to tell you that having relationships with ADHD is easy or that maintaining a career is easily achievable, but I can help you deal with all that comes with it. It is important to understand your body as a woman with ADHD, and this includes understanding your hormones and how they affect your disorder.

This workbook is going to facilitate your relationships, whether with your family, friends, or at work. It is going to help you understand why your house is not always decluttered and organized. I can write about the reason why you live the way you do, but if I do not offer solutions to your problem, this workbook would not serve its sole purpose; to help you live a better life with your ADHD.

The practical tips and exercises are going to help you and your partner live a more peaceful life. From daily self-care routines to factual meal-prep tips and anything in between, you are soon going to feel you are on top of your mental and physical health. Forget about the blame and weight you have put on yourself for being who you are all this time. You are going to appreciate yourself and thrive using the skills you have, developing the ones that need some work, and learning to handle the rest.

By the end of this workbook, you are going to stop expecting so much from yourself and celebrate yourself for everything you accomplish from now on, whether big or small. Whether your focus is your career or your family, you are going to start appreciating your value in this world, at home, and at your job. If you have felt unappreciated because of your ADHD, this is going to change soon.

If you suffer from anxiety, depression, eating or mood disorders because of your undiagnosed ADHD, you are going to learn to work around your neurodiverse brain and lessen these sufferings. If you have asked yourself; "Why have I not known this before?" you are not to blame. You and most other undiagnosed women have been given a multitude of excuses to make up for their shortcomings because of their ADHD, but never have they been given a proper diagnosis. This has affected them all their lives, and no one better than you know this. This workbook has all the answers you have been looking for this whole time.

Make sure you take notes whenever you need to and mark the sections on this workbook if you want to revisit them later. This goes especially for the tips and exercises you want to go through daily or weekly. If you feel like you need to further elaborate on some of the points mentioned in this workbook or some of the feelings these pages will ignite in you, either with your doctor, therapist, or counselor, make sure you keep a separate journal to take note of these.

Contrary to what you believe, there are skills and techniques you can acquire to hinder the interference caused by your ADHD in your everyday life, and this workbook has it all. It is going to help you with self-reflection, and help you find your comfort in different aspects of your life, be it at a party, at home, with family, or with your partner.

You can take notes whilst reading using a separate journal. If you tried journaling before but failed, this workbook is going to help you with that too. I encourage you to work on the exercises included in this workbook and take note of all the tips that apply to you. If some parts of this workbook do not apply to you, feel free to skip those sections. If any parts of this workbook make you feel uncomfortable or put you under unnecessary stress, make sure you take note of these and speak to your therapist about them. It is expected to feel uncomfortable at the time when reading this workbook, but if the situation gets worse, it is important to seek professional help. The scope of this workbook is to help you reframe your mind and help you understand yourself. However, understanding is not enough. You need to improve the impression you have of yourself and change the way you start and end your day. That is only achieved through a series of changes, structured and tracked changes that can be kept long-term. This is why you need to keep track of the tips that most suit you until they are well engraved in your daily life.

This is not to say that your ADHD will be cured by the end of this, but you are going to learn heaps of information, with practical real-life examples and situations, that is going to make dealing with life with ADHD so much easier. Ultimately, this process is going to be done with compassion and care, and carries no judgment, unlike what you have encountered in your life so far. It is a process that you must go through, but the journey is worthwhile.

CHAPTER 1:
UNDERSTANDING ADHD

Attention deficit hyperactivity disorder is a mental condition that impacts how people behave. People with this disorder may appear restless, struggle to focus and act impulsively. ADHD can affect a person in different areas of their life, including academic and professional success, interpersonal connections, and daily functioning.

ADHD is regarded as a chronic and irreversible condition. When left untreated, it can result in low self-esteem and poor social skills. Adults with this disorder may have low self-esteem, are hypersensitive to criticism, and have increased self-criticism, potentially as a result of receiving more criticism overall.

An early diagnosis can help the child learn skills to cope with their lives, but that will not cure their condition. However, having the right tools to deal with life earlier surely facilitates the process.

Children with ADHD can have trouble focusing or paying attention in class, be hyperactive, and have impulsive behaviors without considering the consequences. Now imagine all of this but in adulthood. Imagine a twenty-five-year-old female struggling to focus during a meeting at work, battling a messy office desk every other day, hyper-focusing on the wrong things at the wrong time, and struggling with social relationships overall. All this, without justification. This is undiagnosed or misdiagnosed ADHD in women.

It is normal for some children to struggle with focus or good behavior and that is often justified if the frequency and intensity are reasonable. But not the same is said for adult women who are expected to keep a clean and tidy home, take care of a family with kids of their own, be successful in their careers, and maintain a social life. If a woman fails in one or more of these areas, she is probably labeled as "all over the place," often phasing out, a failure, and irresponsible. I am sure I do not need to describe these situations in too much detail, as you know them all too well by now.

Before you start pointing fingers, scientific studies have little evidence on the risk factors of ADHD, so it is not very likely that yours was caused by bad parenting, but genetics does play an important role here. Having said this, you may raise the question "Why were my male counterparts given the diagnosis, the justification, and the why for their behavior as kids, and I was not?"

ADHD is highly undiagnosed in adults when compared to the diagnosis made in children, but that is not all. 5.4% of ADHD diagnoses in men is compared to 3.2% of diagnoses in females. This is not because women tend to suffer from the disorder less than men, but it is because the symptoms in both genders are different, with those in boys or men being slightly more prevalent. This makes male ADHD diagnosis easier and available earlier in their life. Women are misdiagnosed or not diagnosed at all up until their late twenties sometimes. This is brought about by the gender differences in how symptoms are displayed in men and women, or better yet in boys and girls.

Anxiety, depression, and sleep disturbances are some of the common diagnoses given to women before being diagnosed with ADHD. It is only when a female encounters problems at home, at work, and in her family, that a diagnosis is made, and this would mean that she would have lived her teenage and early adulthood thinking she suffers from anything other than ADHD. I am sure these situations resonate well with you.

The more demands and expectations a woman have, the more prominent her undiagnosed ADHD symptoms become. The disorder affects the areas of the brain that aid in task planning, concentration, and execution. Depending on which type of disorder you suffer from, symptoms may differ. Most commonly, those with ADHD would be inattentive, lack focus, have poor time management, weakened impulse control, overly exaggerated emotions, hyperfocus, and hyperactivity.

Different Types of ADHD

Different approaches speak of different types of ADHD in different ways and some state there are more than just three types of this disorder. However, for easy reference, the following are the three main types and a brief explanation of each:

- **Hyperactive and Impulsive Type**

    Individuals with this type often find themselves in constant movement, talking excessively, interrupting others, and finishing their sentences. This type is more common in men, and easier to diagnose than the other types because it is highly noticeable.

- **Inattentive Type**

    This type is more common in women and was previously known as ADD (attention deficit disorder). Individuals suffering from this type would have a weakened working memory, get easily distracted, and find it difficult to sustain attention or follow instructions.

- **Combined Type**

    As the name implies this type would have a combination of the two types mentioned above. For someone to be diagnosed with this particular type, they would have to display six symptoms from the inattentive type and six from the hyperactive-impulsive type.

To better understand ADHD, the below is going to explain the symptoms of the different ADHD types. Keep in mind that the "Combined Type" needs to have 6 symptoms of each of the two other types.

Hyperactive-Impulsive Type Symptoms

- Talkative
- Impulsive
- Impatient
- Often interrupting others
- Often seen by others as "always on the go"
- Struggles with relaxation and unwinding
- Finishing others' sentences and shouting out answers before the question is even finished
- Taking over other people's tasks to finish them themselves

Inattentive Type Symptoms

- Struggle to focus
- Difficulty finishing tasks
- Daydreaming
- Lose track of tasks and conversations regularly
- Does not pay close attention to detail
- Difficulty in following instructions
- Forgetful with daily tasks, such as chores and errands
- Avoid tasks that require mental effort such as compiling reports or filling out forms.
- Difficulty in organizing tasks
- Distracted easily
- Easily loses things

Causes of ADHD

Researchers are examining the root cause and risk factors for ADHD to improve management and lower the likelihood that someone would get it.

The following are some of the possible causes of ADHD to date:

- Genetic Factor

    No one gene or set of genes has been pinpointed as the disorder's root cause. However, it is crucial to remember that families of those with ADHD frequently experience the same issues.

    Scientists are still examining whether certain genes, particularly those connected to the neurotransmitter dopamine, have an impact on the emergence of ADHD.

    According to a research source, ADHD may be caused by a drop in dopamine levels. Dopamine aids in the transmission from one nerve to another in the brain. It contributes to the onset of emotions and reactions.

    Other studies talk about the structural variation in the brain. According to research, people with ADHD have a smaller volume of gray matter. The brain regions that aid in communication, self-regulation, decision-making, and motor control are included in the gray matter.

- Brain Injury

    Children who have experienced a severe head injury are more prone to developing it, although according to recent research, symptoms may not appear for up to ten years.

- Alcohol and Smoking During Pregnancy

    There is not enough data to conclusively prove that maternal prenatal drug use causes ADHD in kids, despite studies suggesting this could be possible via intrauterine effects.

- Early Exposure to Environmental Factors

    According to some studies, children who consumed diets high in added sugar, fat, and sodium and poor in fiber and omega-3 fatty acids were more likely to develop ADHD.

    Coloring chemicals and preservatives in food may cause ADHD, but this connection might only apply to kids who already have a high risk of developing the disorder.

- Preterm Delivery and Low Birth Weight

    Between 34 and 40 weeks of gestation, different varieties of brain cells show significant growth and development. Because of their underdeveloped brain, preterm babies are more likely to develop ADHD, but not enough research has been done to confirm this.

All things considered, the evidence appears to support the idea that genetic and neurological factors influence the development of ADHD more than social or environmental ones. It is believed that the genes you get from your parents play a key role in developing ADHD because it tends to run in families. However, the inheritance pattern for ADHD is not simple and therefore cannot be assumed to be due to a single genetic defect.

Co-existing Conditions With ADHD

About 60 to 70% of individuals with the disorder also have a comorbid illness, such as drug misuse, anxiety, or a mood disorder. Although the following information may not need too much introduction for a woman with ADHD like yourself, it is important to understand the co-occurring conditions with ADHD. This is going to help you understand yourself and your ADHD better, giving you the explanation, you were looking for and is now long overdue.

More than two-thirds of people with ADHD also have one or more additional medical conditions. These other problems may be overshadowed by the signs of the disorder, which include constant movement and fidgeting, interrupting and dishing out replies, difficulties sitting still, the need for frequent reminders, and so on.

But just as untreated ADHD can pose difficulties in daily life, untreated related conditions can also result in unnecessary suffering in people with ADHD and their families. While any disease can coexist with ADHD, some disorders are more likely to occur.

The following are some of the most common co-existing disorders often found with ADHD:

- **Oppositional Defiant Disorder (ODD)**

    Sufferers would usually argue a lot, lose their temper, refuse to follow rules, blame, and annoy others on purpose. In most cases, people with ODD would be angry individuals, who are also resentful, vindictive, and spiteful.

- **Mood Disorder**

    Extreme mood swings are a marker of mood disorders. Mania, bipolar disorder, and depression are examples of mood disorders.

    According to some studies, about 47% of adults with ADHD also experience depression. ADHD typically manifests first, followed by sadness. Genes and the environment may both play a role.

    Bipolar disorder is a severe condition marked by periods of mania, abnormally high mood, and excessive activity, contrasted by episodes of clinical depression. Up to 20% of people with ADHD may exhibit indications of this illness. Bipolar disorder can harm relationships, cause issues at work, and even result in suicide if untreated.

- **Anxiety**

    Patients with anxiety disorders worry excessively about various things, which can leave them feeling tense, jittery, exhausted, and unable to fall asleep soundly.

- **Sleep Disorder**

    Sleep issues may be a sign of ADHD, exacerbated by ADHD, or make ADHD symptoms worse. When you feel like your brain is working like a motor, you would think that falling asleep at night would be an easy task to do. That is only to realize that as you rest your head on the pillow, you start ruminating on the million things you could have said, you could have done, and that one embarrassing moment you had when you were five years old. This leaves you with a restless mind and body; a restless mind and body that will have to face another eight to ten hours of work and a million other things to do during the day.

You may remember having this sleeping issue as a child. This is accurate and true because most parents of children with diagnosed ADHD report that their children have a sleeping problem.

- Substance Abuse

According to research, children with ADHD are more likely to start smoking cigarettes at a young age before moving on to drinking alcohol and then using drugs.

Adolescents with the disorder are more likely to smoke, and adults also smoke more frequently and report having a harder time stopping.

Youth with the disorder are twice as likely to develop a nicotine addiction as those without the disorder. Difficulty in stopping this bad habit can have adult ADHD individuals abusing different illegal substances as they grow older, having more financial leeway and easier accessibility.

- Conduct Disorder

Some people discover they are unable to refrain from breaking the law, acting violently toward others, engaging in physical altercations, bullying, or even stealing. People with these difficulties can receive treatment, but experts advise starting early to ensure the course of action suits the interests of the sufferer and their family.

- Eating Disorder

The prevalence of obesity, bulimia, and binge eating is higher in people with ADHD due to poor self-control and impulsivity, despite the absence of studies focusing on women, girls, and eating disorders associated with ADHD.

Self-control issues and a lack of awareness of inner states like hunger and fullness are frequent features of ADHD. Planning and consistency are necessary to break bad eating habits like bingeing or overeating, but these traits are hampered by the executive functioning issues linked to ADHD.

ADHD in Women - The Challenge

Women with ADHD may go their entire lives without receiving a diagnosis. This diagnosis gap exists in part because the disorder was once assumed to mostly afflict men, but it is also because women typically exhibit less pronounced or socially disruptive symptoms than men.

Due to the possibility that their symptoms may differ from those of men, women with ADHD frequently go without a diagnosis. Men are more likely to develop hyperactive-impulsive ADHD, which can make them nervous, restless, disruptive, chatty, impulsive, impatient, and moody. Women, on the other hand, usually have inattentive ADHD, which makes it challenging to concentrate, pay attention to details, maintain organization, listen, and recall information.

The underdiagnosis and misdiagnosis of ADHD in women may be significantly influenced by gender bias. When they manifest in women, some of the symptoms of inattentive ADHD, such as shyness or impulsivity, are sometimes seen as personality qualities rather than symptoms.

According to studies, there are a few minor distinctions between men and women with ADHD, however, they are often more similar than different. Girls typically have fewer coping mechanisms and worse self-efficacy than boys during adolescence. Additionally, compared to men, women exhibit fewer externalizing symptoms like hostility but more despair and anxiety.

Below are some of the major differences in ADHD diagnosis between the genders:

Women	Men
Less likely to be given a diagnosis, especially in their childhood	More likely to be given a diagnosis earlier in their lives
Often experience anxiety and low self-esteem	Display disruptive behaviors and often act out
More inattentive	Hyperactive and impulsive
Display verbal aggression	Display physical aggression

In contrast to signs and symptoms of other conditions, ADHD symptoms in women are usually seen as character qualities instead of how a disorder displays itself. For instance, a woman may be described as talkative, forgetful, or dreamy.

Later in adulthood, a woman may seek assistance for her symptoms only to be given a depression or anxiety diagnosis. The good news is that more women may now access the necessary care due to growing awareness of the signs of ADHD in women, and this book is going to help you do just that.

The overwhelming and worn-out sensations experienced by men and women with ADHD are similar. Chronic stress, feelings of inadequacy, low self-esteem, and psychological suffering are widespread.

In today's society, women are typically expected to take care of others. Taking care of others might seem almost impossible when things feel out of control and it is hard to plan and organize because of ADHD.

Additionally, this cultural pressure may significantly amplify a woman's feelings of inadequacy. Adults with undiagnosed or improperly diagnosed ADHD often struggle to focus, miss deadlines, and have problems with organizing the elements of their everyday life.

EXERCISE:

The following are some of the ways ADHD is displayed in your everyday life and the common scenarios you may experience. Under each scenario, you will find a tick box. This is here for you to reflect on and decide whether this particular situation happens to you. If it does, you will need to tick the scenario and scale the frequency of it, by jotting down a number in the designated space, with 1 meaning it does not happen too often and 5 meaning it happens frequently. If a scenario does not apply to you, you can skip it and move on to the next scenario.

Relationship Scenario:

☐ You often wish you could do the things that other people do and be a better friend, lover, or mother. For instance, you probably wish you could make cookies, remember birthdays, and be on time for dates.

Scale 1-5:

☐ People could assume you do not care if you cannot perform the tasks that society expects women to perform.

Scale 1-5:

Social Life Scenario:

☐ You may have been labeled a tomboy as a child due to your boundless energy and desire for activity.

Scale 1-5:

☐ Because social norms appear to be complex as an adult, maintaining friendships can be challenging. People may claim that you talk more than any other person they know of.

Scale 1-5:

☐ Despite your talkativeness, you might not look forward to going to parties and other social events because they make you feel uncomfortable and awkward.

Scale 1-5:

☐ In talks, whether you are the one speaking or the subject is particularly interesting to you, your mind tends to wander.

Scale 1-5:

Work Scenario:

☐ Being at work is challenging. The commotion and people make it challenging to complete work. Because you can only work when it is peaceful and everyone else has left, you may opt to stay late or come in early.

Scale 1-5:

☐ There are a lot of files on your desk at work. It only stays clean for one or two days, despite your best efforts.

Scale 1-5:

☐ Even though you know you are just as brilliant, you could feel upset as an adult when your schoolmates succeeded but you feel like you did not.

Scale 1-5:

Everyday Life Scenario:

☐ When you have ADHD, it could seem like your days are spent limiting disasters and accommodating requests rather than making progress toward your objectives. You might experience excruciating despair and rage at not living up to your potential.

Scale 1-5:

☐ It often feels like you are sinking into paper; in your car, at home, at work, and even in your handbag. You have the unsettling impression that beneath all the paper are overdue debts and neglected tasks.

Scale 1-5:

☐ You frequently get behind on your bills and do not feel financially organized.

Scale 1-5:

☐ You frequently overspend to make up for other issues. For instance, you might get a new dress if you do not have a pristine outfit to go to an office party.

Scale 1-5:

☐ You buy a pricey gift to make up for forgetting someone's birthday.

Scale 1-5:

☐ Shopping makes you feel better in the moment, but when the credit card bill comes, you regret it.

Scale 1-5:

☐ You might invest a lot of time, money, and research into finding organizational products, yet you might not use them. Scale 1-5:

☐ Due to how cluttered and untidy your house is, you could feel ashamed to invite guests around.

Scale 1-5:

☐ You can feel overwhelmed in grocery stores and struggle to decide what to buy.

Scale 1-5:

☐ Despite taking longer than most individuals to shop, you frequently forget a necessary component for a dinner.

Scale 1-5:

Results:

Total ticked scenarios:	Scale values added:

There are nineteen scenarios and if you ticked more than half of these with a scale of three and higher in most of them, your ADHD is likely interrupting your daily life.

The interruptions, as you may have noticed, are happening in different but important aspects of your life. From now on, it is important to take note either in this workbook or in a separate journal, of the areas that you feel need work. This will either mean in your relationships, at work, or on yourself. The strategies and tips to follow, are easy to navigate and apply where they are required.

Diagnosing ADHD

The procedure of determining whether you have ADHD or not involves numerous steps. It cannot be diagnosed with a single test, and many other conditions, including anxiety, depression, and sleep issues, can exhibit similar symptoms. A medical exam is one of the steps in the procedure to rule out other conditions that have similar symptoms. A checklist for assessing ADHD symptoms and gathering information from parents, teachers, and oneself are typically part of the process of diagnosing the disorder. An ADHD diagnosis can only be made based on the existence of symptoms that have developed over time. Although ADHD can be identified at any age, this condition first manifests in young children. The symptoms must be present before the person is twelve years old to make the diagnosis.

Who Can Make a Diagnosis?

Although a general practitioner cannot formally diagnose ADHD, they can talk with you about your worries and, if necessary, recommend you for a specialist assessment. A psychiatrist and a neurologist are both qualified professionals who can diagnose this condition. Alternatively, a psychotherapist or a psychologist can perform tests and assessments that will help them reach a diagnosis. Other physicians may be able to diagnose you but it is important to choose a healthcare professional that is experienced in diagnosing adult ADHD.

Criteria for Diagnosis

Some of the criteria a general practitioner may use to recommend you for additional evaluation by a mental health specialist are as follows:

1. Since your symptoms cannot be attributed to a mental health condition, ADHD could be the cause of your symptoms.
2. You were not given an ADHD diagnosis as a child, but you have been experiencing symptoms ever since.
3. These symptoms have a significant impact on your day-to-day life, such as if you struggle in intimate relationships or perform poorly at work.
4. Symptoms are present in more than one setting, meaning symptoms are experienced at work, at home, or in school if you are still studying.
5. Symptoms have been present from the age of twelve onwards.

The Assessment

The doctor may want to know more about your symptoms; when they started, and where they occur, that is if at work, at home, and so on. They will also evaluate how they affect you in your day to day and if you have any history of ADHD in your family. To finalize their assessment, specialists may need to conduct a physical examination and a series of interviews with you and with your significant others.

Because there is considerable debate over whether the symptoms used to identify ADHD in children and teenagers also apply to adults, diagnosing the disorder in adults is more challenging. If an adult exhibits five or more of the inattentiveness symptoms or five or more of the hyperactivity and impulsivity symptoms described in the diagnostic criteria for children with ADHD, they may in some situations be diagnosed with the disorder. Your current symptoms will be discussed with the professional as part of their evaluation. A diagnosis of the disorder in adults, however, cannot be established under the current diagnostic guidelines unless your symptoms have been present since childhood. Additionally, no other condition must be able to explain the symptoms better. Your consultant may want to review your old school records and speak with your parents, teachers, or anybody else who knew you well when you were a child if you have trouble recalling whether you experienced issues as a child. A visit to the clinic or a quick conversation with the sufferer cannot accurately diagnose ADHD. A complete life history must be taken by the consultant because the patient may not always display symptoms during the appointment.

When making an ADHD diagnosis, co-occurring disorders must be taken into account. Adults must also have symptoms that have a moderate impact on a variety of facets of their lives to receive a diagnosis.

As a guideline, doctors use the diagnostic and statistical manual for mental disorders. It is important to receive an official diagnosis from a licensed practitioner. Together with a series of diagnostic tools, doctors will conduct a set of interviews, and knowing what to expect can make you feel more at ease during this process. An in-depth history of the person is given during a structured or semi-structured interview, which is the most crucial component of a thorough ADHD examination. To enhance dependability and reduce the likelihood that a new interviewer might reach a different result, the interviewer uses a predetermined, standardized set of questions. The physician covers a wide range of subjects, goes into great depth about pertinent concerns, and asks follow-up questions to make sure all important topics are addressed. The examiner will go over the diagnostic standards for ADHD and assess how many of them, both currently and going back to childhood, apply to the subject. The extent to which these ADHD symptoms are interfering with the person's life will also be determined during the interview. The examiner will also perform a thorough evaluation to check for any additional mental conditions that could be present and could be mistaken for ADHD or that frequently coexist with it. More than two-thirds of persons with the disorder have one or more co-occurring disorders, according to studies, as it seldom occurs alone. The most prevalent ones include drug use disorders, depression, and anxiety-related conditions. Failure to address co-existing disorders frequently fails to treat ADHD. More importantly, failing to recognize that ADHD symptoms are a side effect of depression, anxiety, or another mental disease may lead to the wrong course of therapy for the patient. Sometimes, however, treating ADHD will take care of the other disease, eliminating the need to manage it separately.

A written summary or report will be completed at the end of the evaluation, and the clinician will give the person and family their diagnostic opinions regarding ADHD as well as any other psychiatric disorders or learning disabilities that may have been discovered during the course of the evaluation. After reviewing treatment options, the clinician will work with the patient to develop a strategy for an effective medical and psychological intervention. Following that, the clinician will consult with the patient's primary care doctors as required.

ADHD is a condition with considerable costs and burdens. Early identification and care can slow the progression of the condition and lessen its long-term effects. Compared to adults who exhibit signs of ADHD but do not have a diagnosis, adults with an ADHD diagnosis have greater functioning, a better quality of life in terms of their health, and higher levels of self-esteem.

Treatment

The most effective treatment plans for ADHD are multimodal ones, which combine several various, complementary modalities to lessen symptoms.

The following would be an appropriate formula for treating this condition:

1. Medication

   This is subject to your treating physician and all prescribed medication should be taken as prescribed by your doctor. It can be challenging to decide whether to use medication to treat the symptoms of ADHD or not. It is of utmost importance to discuss any side effects with the doctor and inform them if you believe you need to stop or modify your medication. You, more than anyone, know how the medication is making you feel. Your doctor will go through how long you should receive therapy, although, in many circumstances, it is given as long as it is effective.

2. Behavioral Treatment, Counseling, and Therapy

   Another way of treating ADHD may be behavioral management for women. This incorporates more lifestyle support as well as cognitive behavioral therapy (CBT); a kind of mental health care that concentrates on the thoughts and actions that take place right now. This method is distinct from conventional psychoanalytic therapy, which involves revisiting and reprocessing the early life events that may have contributed to contemporary emotional issues. CBT differs from these earlier therapies in that its objectives and strategies are made explicit and, as a result, are measurable for every patient. Some CBT programs are designed to assist people in overcoming their challenges with daily executive functions, which are essential for time management, organization, and long- and short-term planning. Other programs concentrate on impulse control, stress management, and emotional self-regulation. Despite not being expressly created to address the symptoms and impairments associated with ADHD, women who are using CBT for comorbid illnesses such as depression and anxiety may find this therapy useful for their ADHD symptoms.

3. Mindfulness and Meditation

For some time, researchers have discussed the benefits of utilizing meditation to treat ADHD, but it has always been unclear if people with the disorder could practice it, particularly if they are hyperactive. Because of mindfulness' adaptability and flexibility, you can customize your approach and make it work for you. The practice of meditation is crucial, but the most essential thing is to practice mindfulness every day, observing where your attention is directed even when you are going about your everyday activities.

4. Diet

Some ADHD sufferers find relief from alternative forms of treatment, such as avoiding specific foods. A balanced diet should be followed by those who have ADHD although you should not stop eating any specific food groups before consulting a doctor. Some people may observe a connection between certain food kinds and worsening ADHD symptoms. If so, record your eating and drinking habits as well as any subsequent behavior in a journal. Talk to your doctor about it, and they could suggest a dietician. This workbook has further tips and exercises concerning diet and how it affects your ADHD as a woman.

5. Exercise

    By raising levels of the neurotransmitters dopamine and norepinephrine, which are key regulators of the concentration system, exercise reduces ADHD symptoms. You can increase the basal levels of dopamine and norepinephrine by engaging in regular physical exercise because it encourages the development of new receptors in certain parts of the brain. In the arousal area of the brain stem, exercise also helps maintain norepinephrine balance.

6. Vitamins and Supplements

    Although there is no evidence to support this, several studies have shown that taking supplements of omega-3 and omega-6 fatty acids may help. Before taking any supplements, it is advised to see a doctor because some of them may interact with medications in unpredictable ways or reduce their effectiveness. Keep in mind that some supplements should not be used for an extended period since they might build up to high enough concentrations in your body to become dangerous.

It requires strategy, organization, patience, and study to find the ADHD approach that works best for you. Thankfully you stumbled on this workbook, the source that has all the possible self-help tips you need to manage your ADHD as an adult.

Your approach to treating it should be a holistic one, keeping an open mind along the way, knowing you are going to find what works for you.

CHAPTER 2:
COPING WITH ADHD

There are plenty of ways you could cope with ADHD, but the goal is not only to survive but to take control of your condition. The idea behind this workbook is to provide you with heaps of practices and tips you could use. What may work for you might not work for others and that is fine. At any point, if you come across information or advice that does not apply to you, feel free to move forward to the next tip, strategy, or exercise. Apart from medication and professional therapy, there are plenty of other ways you could manage your ADHD.

Mindfulness and Self-Awareness

Paying attention and maintaining self-control are everyday struggles for many individuals with ADHD. So, it makes sense that an extremely effective and priceless natural treatment for ADHD would involve some type of attention training that simultaneously improves self-control. Many religious traditions use meditation or mindfulness practices. Vipassana meditation, for instance, is a type of mindfulness practice found in Buddhism. However, mindfulness is not always spiritual or religious. It entails paying attention to your thoughts, feelings, and physical sensations, or, to put it another way, increasing your awareness of what is happening around you at any given time. It may be a strategy for promoting well-being, particularly psychological wellness. Similar methods have been employed to treat chronic pain, stress, and mood problems as well as to control blood pressure.

Contrary to many ADHD therapies, mindfulness fosters the person's innate abilities. Strengthening your capacity for self-observation, focusing attention, and creating new connections with stressful situations, help you regulate your attention better. In other words, it trains you to pay attention to focusing and can also increase emotional intelligence so that individuals don't respond recklessly. For those who have ADHD, that's frequently a serious issue.

For instance, you could find that while you're driving, your thoughts start to stray to an errand you need to do later that day. Thinking of the many things you have to do on the day can cause you to lose focus on the road. So being mindful in such a situation will benefit you mentally and prevent accidents. Many people engage in mindfulness when they are eating, walking, showering, or even cleaning the house. You may utilize the method whenever you want after you grow used to checking in with yourself and your body. The fundamental method is pretty straightforward.

Concentration and emotional control are two things that mindfulness may aid with. Additionally, it can help in making decisions, controlling stress levels, and significantly enhancing interpersonal interactions and communication. The fact that mindfulness may be used as a technique at any time is one of its finest features. Include short routines where you check in with your body, your breath, and your surroundings throughout the day. Although some people practice sitting meditation for 30, 60, or more minutes at a time, for someone with ADHD, it may be unattainable or daunting. There will be more unplanned awareness as you practice mindfulness. As you read this you may be brainstorming how are you going to go about being mindful of your surroundings, so here is where you should start.

Exercise:

What can you see around you? List between 3 to 5 things.

_____

_____

_____

_____

_____

What are the things you can reach out and touch? List 3 things.

_____

_____

_____

What are the things you can hear? List 3 things.

_____

_____

_____

What are the things you can smell? List 2 things.

_____

_____

What is the one thing you can taste?

_____

_____

You may practice mindfulness at any moment, even while engaging in social interaction. Any time during the day, even for a short while, turning on the mind-awareness state is an excellent practice. In essence, it involves putting aside your busy thoughts and focusing on what is going on right now. The mind is naturally prone to distraction. Mindfulness improves your capacity for concentration. And the emphasis on refocusing, on avoiding the mind's inclination to wander, is what makes this strategy so beneficial for someone with ADHD.

The following are some additional things you can do while you practice mindfulness:

- Find your definition of a comforting snack and munch on it while you engage your senses.
- If you are outdoors, opt for nature and look around. Practicing the self-awareness exercise above will be easy if you are in a park or outdoors.
- Light your favorite candle as you sit quietly.
- Use a fidget toy as you sit down and practice mindfulness.
- If you love cooking, try focusing on the act of slicing veggies and performing one task at a time.
- If you are a person who enjoys gardening, use this hobby to focus on repotting plants.
- If you are the creative type and enjoy pottery-making for example, try focusing on the pottery wheel as the clay is formed with your bare hands.

Overcoming Indecisiveness

Your decision-making may be impacted by ADHD in several ways. Impaired working memory, inattention, and distractibility are among the classic causes. This indicates that some individuals struggle to keep a variety of ideas and concepts in their minds long enough to conclude. It is common while making decisions to also need to weigh your possibilities. Sufferers could find it challenging to sort through too many options. They could spend so much time pondering that they are unable to make a choice. Results of prior selections may cause unfavorable emotions or a lack of confidence in one's ability to make wise choices. This may make it difficult for you to make other choices. Another issue sufferers experience is opting for choices that yield immediate rewards or satisfaction. The quickest decision is not always the best one. Moreover, one may find it difficult to predict the outcome or assess it before making a choice and this does not help in the decision-making process.

All of these struggles experienced when making a decision, lead to what is known as 'decision fatigue' which leaves the individual with a lot of pressure to make a decision, often without concluding.

The following are some decision-making tips that are ADHD-friendly and will help you makes important decisions faster with less overthinking:

- Define the challenge and the outcome you wish to have. This is going to get your mind to filter the options and help you focus on the decision you wish to make.
- Write everything down, in whatever format works for you; spreadsheet, chart, or anything that works for you. This will help improve your working memory, something you know you struggle with. Writing things down will also help you visualize your options and a possible outcome.
- List the pros and cons of any decision. If you have more than one decision you need to make, list them separately, with a deadline if applicable, and all the possible options available for each. Sometimes seeing all the negatives of one choice written down will make it so much easier to choose.
- Decision-making requires focus, concentration, and deep thoughts. If you are surrounded by noise and clutter, making a decision will prove harder than expected. Find a quiet room or space to help you focus.
- If your decisions are not bound by a deadline, make sure you give them one yourself. This will help you to avoid procrastination, something you know how to do all too well.
- Set a limit to your choices. The more choices you have the harder it will be for you to decide.
- Asking for advice is OK. Making decisions can be made easier if you get the assistance of someone you can trust to go through your thoughts and provide feedback.

- If you have had bad experiences with the decision-making process, it may be difficult to feel certain about your choices. However, acknowledging all of your daily successes, no matter how minor, might help you feel more confident.
- Make decisions yourself before they are done on your behalf. If you take too long to make up your mind and you are known for this, it may be the case that you are either not given the choice, to begin with, or because the decision is restricted by a deadline, someone else may decide before you do.
- Leave your focus on significant decisions. You should adopt an approach to reduce unnecessary stress caused by trying to make decisions on less important things. "How?" you may ask. The following method will help you do just that.

Finding the Degree of Uncertainty

Another approach you can use to reach a decision you have been worrying about is finding the degree of uncertainty. This process does not only help you make the right choices but will also help you reduce the amount of time you spend on each decision, lessening the rumination and time taken to decide on somewhat trivial decisions.

Exercise:

These are the steps needed to decide on the degree of uncertainty any given decision may have:

1. Decision:
2. Deadline: (if applicable, if not set one yourself).
3. How important is this decision to you? Scale it from 1 (not so important) to 10 (very important):
4. How high is the risk of you making the wrong choice? Scale it from 1 (not very high risk) to 10 (very high risk):

5. Take some time to think about the risks associated with this decision and list them here. Think along the lines of "What will happen if ...":

_____
_____
_____
_____
_____
_____
_____
_____
_____
_____

Example: There is much more at stake when choosing the right job or career as opposed to choosing your outfit for tomorrow at work. So, it is understandable for you to spend time researching different career options or finding the right job for you. But it is not reasonable for you to spend hours staring at your wardrobe thinking of all the possible wrong combinations of pants and shirts you could put on tomorrow morning.

List the pros and cons of this decision. For example, if you accept an offer or refuse, or if you pick this house or the other.

Pros:

_____

_____

_____

_____

_____

_____

_____

Cons:

_____

_____

_____

_____

_____

_____

_____

List the consequences of your "wrong" choice for this decision.

_____

_____

_____

_____

_____

If you have given this decision a high score meaning it is risky to make the wrong choice, it means you need to spend more time because the degree of uncertainty is low. A wrong choice could potentially affect you negatively.

The higher the risk = The lower your level of uncertainty should be.

After you have evaluated the situation as per the above steps, you need to assign the time you will spend on making this decision. Always keep in mind the deadline if you have one for this decision.

The time needed to finalize this decision:

_____

_____

Everyone with ADHD is different, and for some people, making decisions might be difficult. But you can create methods to make the process simpler and more efficient. The takeaway from this exercise is to always allow room for mistakes but determine to what extent will that be. Lastly, the goal of this is to leave perfectionism for the more important decisions.

agement

For some people, time management issues are the ones that give them the greatest pain and difficulty. The main issue with ADHD is executive dysfunction. These deficiencies account for the difficulties that individuals with ADHD experience. Our executive functions assist us in taking the actions we know we ought to. People with ADHD tend to get trapped in the here and now and struggle to make decisions that will help them in the future.

In life, there is a never-ending stream of stimuli begging for our attention and objectives requiring our efforts. While some of these stimuli and tasks are enjoyable and simple, others are tedious, difficult, or draining. Some of them reward us immediately, while others need us to take action now to reap rewards later. An effort should be made to achieve a balance between taking in the moment and planning for tomorrow. To create a space where we can consider our alternatives and come to the optimal conclusion, one must struggle to disengage from the temptations and distractions of the present.

People with ADHD are more focused on the present than other people are. They are greatly affected by their environment. Those without ADHD are better able to block out outside influences. Executive functions can be used by neurotypical people to make decisions depending on their objectives. People with ADHD are less motivated by rewards and punishments that are farther away. On Monday, a deadline on Friday is meaningless. They do not go to bed at 10 p.m. whilst also setting the alarm for tomorrow's 6 a.m. People with ADHD are aware that acting sooner rather than later is preferable, but they struggle to carry this through. Many individuals with the disorder are unaware of future events and repercussions since they do not become apparent on their mental radars until much later. Even if a task is on their to-do list, they lack the drive to do it. As a result, they become unduly dependent on the impending deadline pressure and are free to put off doing things.

Planning, attention, and forward-thinking are necessary for time management. Your life could become less frustrating if you understand these techniques and start adopting them.

Here are some of the most common struggles with time management for ADHD sufferers:

- Forgetting tasks
- Not allocating enough time for what you planned to do.

- Having to complete what to you is a boring task.
- Not allowing enough transition time if tasks include traveling or involve you being outside the house.
- Not enough navigating time is available to complete tasks. There is not much flexibility.
- Take on more many tasks than you can handle.

Time Blindness

The inability to perceive time passing or remember specific memories' times or events is known as time blindness. It is a typical symptom in those with neuro-diverse brains. It may be tough for them to make plans weeks in advance since it is challenging to think that far ahead. Executive functioning includes time management. It entails being aware of time, how much time is left to do a task or activity, and the capacity to gauge the speed of time. Timing issues are strongly correlated with negative behavioral outcomes including impulsivity and inattention, which are the pillars of the ADHD diagnosis. Lack of focus can result in a variety of problems, such as the inability to fulfill obligations or expectations at work or home. A persistent lack of productivity may also irritate co-workers or superiors, leaving persons with ADHD time blindness feeling inadequate and guilty. In essence, the misjudgment of time is a sensory issue rather than a decision.

The following is a reflection exercise aimed at helping you determine whether you struggle with effective time management, how often this happens to you, and if you need to action this immediately. The following are some scenarios in different settings. Under each scenario, you will find a tick box. This is here for you to reflect on and decide whether this particular situation happens to you. If it does, you will need to tick the scenario and scale the frequency of it, by jotting down a number in the designated space, with 1 meaning it does not happen too often and 5 being it happens frequently. If this scenario does not apply to you, you can go ahead and skip it and move on to the next one.

☐ You arrive late to events or parties.

Scale 1-5:

☐ You are not able to stay organized at work or in school.

Scale 1-5:

☐ You struggle to complete tasks within a set timeframe at work.

Scale 1-5:

☐ You get distracted when you need to move from one task to the next.

Scale 1-5:

☐ You always pick your children up late from school or their extracurricular activities.

Scale 1-5:

☐ You forget you had a deadline due or forget the task completely. Scale 1-5:

☐ You put paying the bills or setting doctor's appointments off every time they are due.

Scale 1-5:

☐ You underestimate how long a task will take you to complete. scale 1-5:

☐ Your intentions are not always in line with your actions.

Scale 1-5:

☐ You feel as if you are a disappointment or failure to others while you work on the task assigned.

Scale 1-5:

☐ You are often labeled as lazy.

Scale 1-5:

Results:

Total ticked scenarios:	Scale values added:

If you ticked half or more of these whilst having a high overall score, it is very likely that you are struggling with time blindness and need to work on externalizing time and adopting better time management techniques.

The following are some tips you can start using today to help manage your time better:

- Identify the areas of your life being affected by time blindness, for example highly affected at work, but not so much at home. The above exercise facilitates this.
- Start your time management routine with small tasks. Each task you complete will boost your motivation.
- List down the tasks you have due and break down the tasks into smaller ones.
- Set up morning and evening routines.
- Organize your space in a way that everything you may need is readily available to you.
- Keep a decluttered and more organized space.
- Prepare things the night before, and this includes, your lunch, your outfit for the day, your gym bag, and whatever else you may need to take with you before you dash out the door.
- Plan a morning routine and stick to it without adding anything further.
- Plan for short breaks during the day. This will come in handy especially if you struggle to maintain focus for extended periods.
- Change your work environment to make it work for you. If you find that your phone distracts you every time a notification pops up put it on DND mode. If you work in an open office, but the chaos makes it harder for you to work, ask if using headphones is allowed at your work.

- Plan for the unexpected. When planning for a task allow some buffer time for what you originally planned. This also works for making it to appointments and events on time.
- Try taking note of the time taken to complete a task the next time you need to do it. With concrete data in hand, you will be able to manage your time better.
- Try setting a bedtime and abide by it. This should be incorporated into your evening routine as well.
- Incorporate physical exercise and healthy eating habits into your lifestyle.
- Keep someone you trust accountable for the tasks planned the next day.
- Do not commit to activities or tasks you know you do not have the time for.
- Leave encouraging notes for yourself to help keep you motivated through this change.
- When planning the day for better time management, keep things you should do separate from the things you want to do.
- Externalise time. Use external instruments, starting with as many clocks as you can see.
- Set alerts and reminders if your schedule is packed with commitments to keep you on track. Eliminate low-importance notifications to make the critical ones stand out.

Creating a Practical Time-Management Routine

With a plan in place, you are less likely to deviate from your routine so scheduling time to plan your time-management routine is crucial. Keep the following points in mind whilst planning your routine:

- Plan how much time you will need on this routine regularly.
- Spend 15 to 30 minutes every week on your time-management routine for the coming days. You may need more time at first and that is understandable.
- Do not look at this as a punishment but as part of your self-care routine.

- You do not always have to sit at home to plan a week's worth of tasks. You can do it over lunch break with one of your close friends or take yourself out to a coffee shop while you plan away.
- If you think you will struggle to start planning think of an activity you could add whilst you plan to increase your dopamine levels and keep you focused.
- Try planning for your routine in advance, for example, schedule the planning for Sundays so you know you can start afresh on Monday morning. Having a set plan for the days ahead is more likely to keep you motivated, and goal-oriented.

Exercise:

How will you know your time management routine is working?

Take some time to evaluate your previous week.

Think of the things you struggled with and write them below.

_____

_____

_____

_____

_____

_____

_____

Did you forget to plan your routine a day ahead of time? Y / N

If you forgot, think of ways you can remind yourself next time and write them below.

_____

_____

_____

_____

_____

Scheduling coffee meet-ups or lunch breaks with a trusted friend to help you with this is one way you could do this. Setting a weekly reminder on your phone is another idea.

If you feel like motivation or focus is the issue you are struggling with, think of ways you could add more dopamine to this activity, such as compiling a playlist on your phone to listen to whilst you plan your routine or using a fidget toy that helps you maintain focus.

Have you allowed enough time to transition between one activity and the next? If not, how can you add more transition time to avoid overpacking your day or failing to manage the tasks you had planned for?

_____

_____

_____

_____

_____

Did you find yourself struggling to move more important things around your routine?

Do you think you were flexible enough with your routine?

Reflect on these two questions and write your thoughts below.

_____

_____

_____

_____

_____

_____

Have you experienced time blindness issues during the past week? If yes, how can this be improved? Think of ways you could externalize time to avoid this happening again in the future.

_____

_____

_____

_____

_____

Were you distracted from your routine? What caused you to get distracted? Think of ways you could prevent this next week.

_____
_____
_____
_____
_____
_____

How realistic was your last week's time management routine? Take note of how much time have tasks taken you last week to help you plan better for the upcoming weeks. List the timings below to have records you could come back to.

_____
_____
_____
_____
_____
_____
_____
_____

Managing Stress Through Relaxation

To manage your stress effectively, it would be helpful to be prepared for when you start feeling overwhelmed or under stress. Try having two or three relaxation methods you know work for you. You can try mindful meditation as previously discussed, but that is not the only way to reduce your stress. Here are some other ways you could do that:

1- Progressive Muscle Relaxation (PMR)

   By steadily tensing and then relaxing each muscle, PMR helps to relieve tension and anxiety in the body. This practice is based on the idea that you cannot suffer symptoms of stress while still having a sense of warmth and calm in your body. Through time and repetition, you will learn to recognize when you are feeling tense and develop the techniques to relieve it.

2- Guided Imagery

   To relax your mind, you might practice focused relaxation by concentrating on a particular thing, sound, or sensation. By using guided imagery, you consciously picture a serene scene or location. Through relaxing and being aware, a peaceful state is going to be fostered. The theory is that when you imagine something, your body responds depending on the image in your head. For instance, your body and mind stiffen up when you contemplate stressful scenarios. However, your mind and body tend to relax if you concentrate on pleasant scenarios. You could be better equipped to handle mental, emotional, and physical stress by soothing your body and mind in this manner.

   You do not need any equipment to practice this and all you need is a quiet place and a comfortable sitting position. If you are using an audio recording to facilitate this you may need headphones but that is all you need. You can do this at any time. Various platforms online provide guided imagery recordings. It is best to experiment with a few and find a couple that works for you. Keep these handy when you need them.

Below is how you could do this without audio:

1. Choose a peaceful place to sit or lie down.
2. Shut your eyes. Breathe deeply. Continue this relaxing breathing, during inhalation and exhalation.
3. Think of a serene setting, such as a forested area, a gorgeous mountain range, or a deserted tropical beach. You might also picture your favorite natural setting where you like to unwind.
4. Consider the specifics of the setting. Envision the sights, sounds, and feelings of being in this tranquil, relaxing setting.
5. Imagine a path through your scene. Imagine yourself traveling down the trail while picturing the specifics and noises you hear.
6. Spend some time letting this sink in. Keep breathing deeply.
7. Count to three after 15 minutes. Open your eyes.

You might want to give guided imagery a try whilst doing yoga or progressive muscle relaxation. Your mind can unwind more easily when your body is calm. Do not be concerned with your performance at first. Relax, do not push yourself too hard, and allow the process to unfold naturally. It takes practice to use guided imagery. Start with 5 minutes every day and work your way up from there. Look at pictures or movies on the internet if you have trouble visualizing calm environments. Choose a relaxing setting, then imagine yourself there.

3- Mindful Coloring

The core idea behind mindful coloring is that the process of coloring already-created drawings gives you a chance to put your inner conversation on hold and partake in an activity that ignores the stream of unfavorable ideas that might rule your life. Mindful coloring is intended to provide people the chance to spend some time in a concentrated state while engaging in a creative activity that can have a relaxing, meditative impact.

Exercise:

Find a coloring page that you like. You can buy a coloring book or choose one of the hundreds of free designs available online. Silence your thoughts as you enjoy this relaxing activity while being mindful.

Evaluating your mindful coloring activity

How many times did you catch yourself overthinking during this activity?

_____

_____

Did you find it hard to focus as you were coloring or were you fully engaged in the activity? What made it hard to stay on task? Were there any external distractions that hindered your focus? Write your thoughts below.

_____

_____

_____

_____

_____

_____

Compare how you were feeling before the mindful coloring experience versus now.

_____

_____

_____

_____

What could you do differently next time to improve this mindful coloring experience?

_____

_____

_____

_____

Using Exercise to Help Manage Your ADHD Better

You may already be aware of the positive effects regular exercise has on your mood. A workout does more for someone with ADHD than just making them feel good. Moreover, it can aid with symptom management. Moving your body boosts your energy, enhances your cognition, and helps you feel less confused. It has many of the same effects on your brain as your ADHD medications. However, to get these benefits, you must exercise properly and in the appropriate amounts.

Finding an exercise that fits your lifestyle and sticking with it are key factors. Dopamine is one of the neurotransmitters that are released during exercise and helps with focus and clear thinking. Dopamine levels in the brains of people with ADHD are frequently lower than average. The stimulant medications that are typically prescribed to treat adult ADHD increase the brain's dopamine availability. Understandably, exercise provides many of the same results as stimulant medications.

Here are some of the ways exercise can benefit your ADHD brain:

- It helps with stress and anxiety.
- It increases working memory and executive function.
- It increases the brain's level of neurotrophic factor, the protein in charge of learning and memory. This usually lacks in the ADHD brain.
- It helps maintain a healthy weight.
- It reduces the risk of chronic conditions such as diabetes and heart disease.
- It controls blood pressure and cholesterol levels.
- It helps strengthen bones.
- It enhances your mood and self-esteem.
- It helps prevent the occurrence of certain brain diseases like Alzheimer's disease.

It is recommended that you exercise between 3 to 5 times a week depending on the duration and intensity of the exercise.

If you are having trouble sticking to regular physical activity, below are some ways you can improve that:

- Choose a friend that can keep you accountable.
- Vary your exercise routine from time to time so you do not get bored. Anything from hiking, walking, running, HIIT or gym workouts are great ideas for physical activities you can incorporate into your daily life.
- Use applications on your phone that help you carry out exercises, and track your repetitions and your attendance.
- Start the day with physical activity. This will set your mood up for the day and keep you focused throughout. Ticking off this habit in the morning, means you are less likely to find excuses to avoid doing it later.

- Keep a habit tracker for physical activity in your journal. You could use this for other habits you would like to start sticking to. You can add this little box to your journal. Here is an example:

Habit	Mon	Tue	Wed	Thur	Fri	Sat	Sun
Drink 2 liters of water	X	X	X	X	X		
Go to the gym		X		X		X	
Meditate						X	X

Write your own habits below:

Habit	Mon	Tue	Wed	Thur	Fri	Sat	Sun

If you still struggle to include a workout 5 times a week, here are some ways you can increase movement during the day:

- Include a stretching routine first thing in the morning. You can use this time to meditate or do yoga as well.
- Instead of sitting down throughout your lunch break try going for a walk after having lunch.
- If you can walk or bike to work, or when running errands, do that.
- Offer walking your neighbor's or friend's dog a couple of times a week.
- Split your unwinding evening time and attend a circuit class or spinning class.
- Try wearing a smartwatch that tracks your steps and calories burnt. Although not 100% accurate, this will help keep you motivated and on track.
- Whenever possible, try conducting walking meetings at work instead of sitting in front of your camera or a meeting room. This is usually only suitable for internal casual meetings.
- Choose walks in the park, trekking, or hiking as outings on your days off.
- Try gardening or doing chores around the house, that counts as movement as well.
- Take the stairs, not the lift.
- Park farther away from work or home to add some extra steps.
- Set a reminder on your phone to stand and walk every hour or so.
- Sit on a stability ball instead of a desk chair, even if not for the whole day. This helps strengthen your core while you work.

Adults can pick from a wide range of exercise activities, all of which can improve their capacity to control their ADHD symptoms. For consistency, concentrate on setting aside a section of your day for exercise and make this a habit.

Chapter 3:
IMPROVING RELATIONSHIPS

While the impulsivity, disorganization, and distractibility of ADHD can be problematic in many aspects of an adult's life, these symptoms can be especially harmful in your closest relationships. This is particularly true if you have never received a thorough diagnosis or treatment. You likely experience continual criticism, nagging, and micromanagement.

Romantic Relationships

Nothing you do appears to satisfy your partner regardless of what you do. You neglect your partner or say everything necessary to get them off your back since you do not feel appreciated. You wish your partner would lighten up just a little bit and quit trying to manage every area of your life. It is simple to understand how the emotions on both sides might lead to a negative vicious circle in the relationship.

In contrast to the non-ADHD partner's complaints, nagging, and growing resentment, the ADHD partner feels defensive and withdraws after feeling judged and misunderstood. No one is satisfied in the end. Nevertheless, things do not have to be this way. Understanding how it affects your relationship and how both of you may make more positive and useful decisions about how to handle difficulties and interact with one another can help you create a better, happier relationship.

These are some ways your ADHD impacts your relationships:

- Zoning out during conversations makes others feel ignored, whilst missing out on important details, or forgetting a few moments later.
- Partners or family members feel like they have to clean up after you as you often leave chaos behind.
- Blurting out your thoughts without filtering causes hurt to others.
- You often lose your temper and have difficulty calmly discussing issues.

Below are some of the most important communication skills to be used when conflict arises because of your ADHD:

- Make every effort to calm irrational emotions. Consider what the fundamental issue in your argument is. What is the bigger problem? It is a lot simpler to find a solution after you have found the legitimate issue.
- Do not hold your feelings anymore. Whatever your feelings may be, be honest about them. Bring things to the forefront so you can resolve them together as a couple.
- Do not presume what your other half is thinking. Talk to them instead of ruminating in silence.
- Avoid using criticizing language or asking questions that might make your partner defensive.
- Laugh at the inevitable miscommunications. Laughing eases tension and strengthens your relationship.
- Nonverbal indicators like eye contact, tones of voice, and gestures convey a lot more information than just words. You must speak to your partner face-to-face.
- Try to keep your eyes on the other person while they are speaking. Repeat their words in your head whenever your attention starts to stray.

- Ask the other person a question instead of just blurting out whatever is on your mind.
- As soon as you become aware that your focus has diverted, apologize to the other person and urge them to restate what was just said.
- Regular mindfulness meditation may give you more control over your emotions and stop the emotional outbursts that can be so harmful to a relationship.
- Try using "I" statements and avoid blaming the other party. This will often have them get defensive as it is an instinct.
- Open up about how your symptoms impair your capacity to remember things and other struggles you face in the relationship.
- Be conscious of your tone of voice. As much as your actual words.
- Have at least one potential solution on hand and ask the other person for their thoughts as well.
- Let the other person talk. Monopolizing the conversation will not help you solve the problem; it will just briefly make you feel better. Use active listening techniques.

Apart from effective communication, there are other things you and your partner can employ to avoid conflict. Here are some tips covering ADHD-related conflict from that caused by forgetfulness, to procrastination and anything in between:

- Research and study ADHD symptoms and how it affects relationships.
- Recognize that your ADHD can and will affect your relationships.
- Understand that you are more than your ADHD symptoms. Your symptoms are not your character traits.
- Take responsibility for the role you play in the relationship and understand your contributions to fixing the communication issues you experience.

- Stick to your task division. If one of you is carrying the majority of the load, make a list of tasks and obligations and equalize the workload. You do not have to handle everything by yourself or with your partner.
- If forgetfulness is an issue in your relationship, use a laptop or a smartphone's calendar or reminders. Having a shared calendar for both of you can help you remember commitments with your partner and avoid conflict.
- Bring cash and stick to your shopping list if you tend to overspend.
- Eliminate temptations. Throw away catalogs and unsubscribe from emails from merchants.
- Consider procrastination a quality that can be controlled rather than a personal flaw. If a huge task feels intimidating divide it into smaller ones.
- If mood swings are the reason for most of your fights, know that these can be avoided with a balanced diet, sufficient sleep, and frequent exercise.
- Stick to visual planners and create routines for both of you to get used to.
- Assign tasks and chores and tick them off when completed.

Maintaining Healthy Relationships With Family and Friends

Relationships with friends need verbal communication, attentive listening, and a grasp of nonverbal indicators. Most women with ADHD struggle to regularly use these strategies. Many women struggle to balance their busy lifestyles and maintain strong connections. They need breaks to refocus on their life. They relish the solitude of the evening when they are not required to be with anybody. They nonetheless make excessive promises to get liked because they need connection.

Understanding how your symptoms affect others is the first step in strengthening your relationships with family and friends. Thankfully, there are various approaches you may follow to deal with your difficulties and promote healthy relationships at the same time.

For instance, it might be challenging for people with ADHD to acquire social skills because of their issues with focus, hyperactivity, impulsivity, and mood control. Your actions could be misinterpreted by others. Your lack of focus or impulsiveness could be perceived by your peers as hostility. Finding and maintaining connections with other people may be much more difficult for someone with ADHD who is simultaneously attempting to control their symptoms. You can feel as though you have too many friends. It may be challenging for you to meet your obligations to your friends while also paying attention to them if you have a lot of other things going on. Your friends can get impatient with you over time. They may feel you do not care or that you just do not value them. If you manage to meet up with your friends, you may get bored and feel like you need to leave the table. Your friends may feel that you are inconsistent with socializing or you do not pay enough attention when you meet. This reinforces inconsistency as well. You may forget your best friend's birthday or forget you even decided to meet up at all. Your low self-esteem interferes with forming new friendships or thinking no one wants to be your friend. If you suffer from anxiety, being invited to a party can cause social anxiety and have you to refuse to attend altogether. If depression is an issue, you may find it difficult to get up and get ready to meet up with friends. All of these issues make maintaining healthy friendships very difficult with ADHD.

Some tips to reduce conflict with others include:

- Keep an eye on your actions. Monitor your behavior and what it is you are doing that is affecting your friendships.

- If you are unsure what was said, or if you missed a detail about your next meet-up, ask them to repeat or re-confirm what you think you understood to avoid miscommunication.

- Let them finish talking and do not interrupt.

- Consider how much you value your friendships and what these relationships mean to you. Once you establish that, you will be able to allocate more time for them and invite them for coffee more often because you know they matter to you.

- Take note of your next meet-up in a calendar or in your diary to avoid forgetting. Following through on commitments shows your friends you care and value them.

- Tell them how much you care about them and if you have a great night out, make sure you let them know. This helps them understand you care about them despite your flaws.

- If some of your friends do not know you have ADHD, tell them and explain to them how this may affect your relationship with them. They may understand you better and this could avoid conflict.

- If you feel overwhelmed and cannot handle the situation, be sure to notify your friends and take some time for yourself. This will help avoid further conflict.

- Practice self-care. This could be one of the most important ways you could manage your ADHD symptoms and avoid exhausting yourself. Overall, this will improve your friendships.

Thankfully, you may strengthen your bonds with your friends by making time for them and showing up. Respect their limits and take the time to let them know they are important to you. Taking care of yourself and getting the right therapy for your ADHD will make your relationships healthier.

Building Supportive Networks

Everyone needs trustworthy friends. The difference between surviving and thriving can be found in one's network of friends and family. Everyone needs someone to bounce ideas off of, to share successes with, and to lean on for a hug. Choose the individuals you want to be a part of your network. According to a popular saying, we develop into an average of the five individuals we spend the most time with. Thus, surround yourself with positive individuals who want the best for you. Who motivates you? Who gives you confidence in yourself?

Continually engage with others as you expand your network. Schedule routine meet-ups with them, because you may have the propensity to lose track of time and months, may pass before you know it. Refuse to follow the inclination to isolate yourself. Instead of waiting for an invitation, invite them yourself instead. Giving and receiving go hand in hand in the strongest friendships. Be a good listener and supporter of others. Acknowledge successes and provide suggestions when you can. The probability that someone will be there for you will increase if you are there for them.

EXERCISE:

Try this exercise the next time you find yourself in a conflict or near conflict with a friend, family member, or partner:

What triggered off the argument? List the people involved (close friends, family members, etc). Which of the ADHD symptom you think triggered this argument? (lack of attention, forgetfulness, etc).

_____

_____

_____

_____

_____

How did the argument make you feel? Analyze your emotions and list them below.

_____

_____

_____

_____

_____

What was your reaction to this argument and what was said?

_____

_____

_____

_____

_____

_____

_____

What could you have done differently? Use some of the tips listed above, and pick the ones that are most suitable for your situation. Use the following writing prompts to compare what happened versus what could have been done differently to avoid conflict and build healthy relationships.

What happened?	*What could have been done differently?*
_____	_____
_____	_____
_____	_____
_____	_____
_____	_____

What happened? *What could have been done differently?*

CHAPTER 4:
MANAGING DAILY LIFE WITH ADHD

One of the first stages in managing ADHD symptoms is receiving a diagnosis. Yet, certain habits, systems, and ways of living may all be combined to lessen symptoms even more and promote mindful living.

The following are some of the common ADHD struggles and ways how to overcome these:

Home Organization and Management

People with ADHD sometimes struggle to complete daily chores. They frequently exhibit forgetfulness, disarray, and clutter. Since cleaning appears like such a hardship to neurotypicals themselves, this makes cleaning with ADHD nearly impossible.

Physical clutter, according to research, overwhelms your brain with stimuli and makes it difficult to concentrate on the task at hand. As a result, organizing and cleaning have been associated with reduced anxiety. Being surrounded by clutter may be depressing. Every unorganized piece of paper and article of clothing lying on the floor serves as a small taskmaster to remind you of everything you have yet to accomplish. You may find some much-needed mental serenity by taking the time to clean and arrange your space. You will become more focused and productive when working in a tidy environment. Below are ideas that can help you keep an organized home despite your ADHD.

Starting with cleaning ideas for the neurodiverse:

- Creating a more organized house can help you make better decisions. According to research, making a timetable in advance and scheduling time for chores will help you stick to a regular cleaning regimen. You can observe your progress and tiny victories thanks to a structured plan, which serves as motivation to keep going. Having to clean the whole house once a week can feel overwhelming as that could be a lot of work to do at once. Keeping little cleaning routines can help you create and maintain a clean space the whole time. Set time aside weekly to plan your chore routine depending on the commitments you have during the coming days.
- Write down your cleaning routine and keep it somewhere handy. On your fridge is a great place. List the chores you need to complete. Allow flexibility in case you cannot complete the task on the day.
- Allow enough time for the chore you planned for the day to avoid either panicking for not managing on time or feeling like you failed.
- Stick to your cleaning routine and only complete what you planned to do for the day. Avoid deep cleaning your house every time you have a chore scheduled in your routine. This can become overwhelming.
- Create a cleaning station wherever cleaning needs to be done. If you find yourself using the same 2 or 3 products to clean the bathroom, create a station in the bathroom. Same for the kitchen, laundry room, and so on. Having every item collected in each room will reduce overwhelm and saves you from running around looking for things you would need to complete your chore for the day.
- If you find that cleaning is boring, try incorporating fun activities as you clean. Some ideas could be listening to music or your favorite podcast.
- Schedule 15 minutes twice a day if you think that cleaning for an hour or so is not doable with your ADHD. You can split these up or do 30 minutes at once if it works better for you.
- Tick off once you complete the task and evaluate the progress you have made at the end of the week as you plan for the coming one. Further down you will find a tracker for this. Whilst evaluating the cleaning schedule, ask yourself:

Exercise:

What went well during last week's cleaning routine?

_____
_____
_____
_____

What did I do wrong, and how could this be improved?

_____
_____
_____
_____

Have I utilized the cleaning stations I prepared? If not, what was the reason? Did I find the items I needed to clean?

_____
_____
_____
_____

Have I allocated enough time for what I had planned, and did I manage on time? How can I fix this?

_____

_____

_____

_____

If you find it hard to stick to a cleaning schedule or wish it was simpler, you can include a cleaning chart as well as a schedule. These need to be used alongside each other. Once you complete the task on the schedule you can tick it off. This should help with motivation and accountability. The chart would look like the following, but you can amend it as you please:

Chore	Mon	Tue	Wed	Thur	Fri	Sat	Sun	Score
Vacuum carpets								/7
Make bed								/7
Clear dishwasher								/7
Remove dust								/7
Clean bathrooms								/7

Making your bed every morning is also highly suggested to start the day with a clearer mind and helps keep your bedroom well-organized. If you struggle to do this every day, include it in the chart above and tick it off after you complete it. As you plan the following week's cleaning schedule, take some time to count what you have accomplished during the current week in terms of cleaning. The score will be out of 7 for the whole week. You will notice how much you have accomplished through this method and will help you plan better the following week. A score out of 7 can help you push yourself the following week.

Home Organization Ideas

- To deal with the problem from its roots, be sure to buy only the things you need. Think of how many times you will use this item and if you see yourself using it often then you can buy it. If not, you can leave it on the shelves. This is especially applicable for single-use kitchen items for example.
- Before organizing your space, you need to declutter. Go around each room and separate the things you use from those you do not. Create donation bins for clothes you have not worn in ages and donate them. Be realistic when decluttering things you do not need. Think of the many times you have utilized this item or worn that shirt. Schedule an afternoon for this and plan to only tackle one room at a time. Planning more than that can be overwhelming and discouraging.
- Buy containers ideally transparent ones so you can see what you have stored inside. Jars and baskets are also great for storage. You will need to measure your space before deciding on which storage container will work best for you. In a kitchen, jars and transparent containers work best. In your closet, you may go for baskets as they could work better, but this is all dependent on your liking, on what is practical to you, and ultimately fits the space you have available.
- Label containers and group alike items.
- Keep the items you use often handy. This will avoid you from creating a mess to access them, and having to organize them once more.
- Make it your religion to store items back where they belong otherwise the work you have done today will be in vain the next morning.

- Leave a container or a drawer just for the little knick-knacks. This will be your space for junk items. Make it a point to go through this space once a week to declutter and avoid it getting out of hand.

- If you have kids and have been trying to find a space for all the artwork they bring back from school, use clips to hang them in one place. Try rotating the artwork they bring from time to time. You do have to display their work but not forever.

- Use shower curtain rings to hand things such as scarves, handbags, or kitchen accessories.

- If you find that you dump your shoes, umbrellas, and bags in the entryway, create a storage space just for this. You can do a DIY project or buy readymade storage to sort out things that inevitably need to be next to the door. This can include a space for your incoming mail, wallet, phone charging station, and keys.

- If you find yourself having too much paper clutter, invest in a shredder and go through the pile every few weeks to avoid it getting out of hand. To avoid the clutter in the first place, opt for electronic correspondence instead, including magazines wherever possible. Investing in a scanner is also helpful. You can save scanned electronic copies of important documents and store the physical ones once and for all.

- Hang things instead of occupying counter space. This is helpful mostly in the kitchen, and you may hang knives and tablecloths for example.

- Store items underneath your bed. You can either use the space there is or invest in a built-in storage bed. This can also be done with other storage furniture like an ottoman.

- Store extra plastic bags in a container and keep them handy wherever they are mostly used.

- Separate items by season and store them as such. As soon as winter is over, use vacuum bags to store away your winter blankets and duvets. Put them away somewhere that is not so easily accessible as you will only need them next year.

- If you are a big family or share the household, make sure everyone has a box or space to store their items. This ensures everyone has their space but at the same

- time limits the number of belongings they can have. This will surely help with minimalism and keep clutter to a minimum.
- Be sure to declutter your most used bag once every few days. This will only take you 5 minutes if you do it so often.
- For your kitchen, be sure to check the expiry dates on all your items including fridge items. Make a list of the things that are nearing their date and plan your next week's meal plan with those items. This will reduce food waste, have you eat mindfully for the following days as you would be sticking to a plan, and overall keep your kitchen decluttered.
- Design special storage areas for toys if you have kids. Instill this habit into your kids as well. Make sure you get storage boxes they can utilize to clear their toys.
- For your medicine cabinet, make sure you check the expiry dates and dispose of the expired items adequately.
- Make it a habit to make your bed in the morning and clear your nightstand as well. Allow only the items you use every night, like a book, journal, or reading light.
- If you have multiple electronic devices that have the same information stored, choose one or two you frequently use, sync the information, and dispose of the devices you use less often.
- Take care of your mail especially bills, every week. Store copies of your bills straight away and chose direct debits whenever possible. This will save you from getting fined for late payments and reduce your paper clutter.

Unfortunately, cleaning your house never really ends. You will always need to clean your house as long as you have one. Even if you struggle with organizing, you can manage your ADHD and household cleaning. Just keep in mind to pause what you are doing and refer back to these recommendations whenever you start to feel overwhelmed by cleaning. You do not have to experience stress or overwhelm. All you need are the appropriate skills and a positive attitude. Start easy, simple, and with a strategy. Cleaning the house will be easier if you have these strategies at the forefront.

Emotional Spending

When you are feeling depressed, it is common to treat yourself with something sweet to reward success. Little "perks," meanwhile, could be emotional expenses. If you often feel bad about spending money on items you will not use, you could be an emotional spender, which is more prevalent than you would realize. Purchases driven by emotions, are usually to make yourself feel better. These feelings could include tension and despair as well as joy and celebration. These decisions are taken in the heat of the moment, spending money on items that are not necessary or within your budget. Impulse buying can be triggered by jealousy, guilt feeling, fear, sadness, or simply celebrating achievements.

Here are some tips to overcome impulse buying based on its trigger:

- If you feel jealous of what your friends own as opposed to yourself, you may shop excessively to keep up. Instead, journal every morning listing down the things you are grateful for. Limit the list to 3 things and list them in your journal. This will make you appreciate the things you have instead of wanting more.

Today I am grateful for:

_____

_____

_____

- If you fail to meet a deadline or reach a goal, you may shop to treat yourself. Instead, evaluate the situation and list down the things you could have done differently to avoid failing again. Shopping will only give you temporary satisfaction.

Goal :

Failure :

What are the things I could do differently next time to avoid failure?

_____

_____

_____

_____

- You may turn to shopping if you are feeling anxious. This is used as a temporary distraction. Try taking a 15-minute walk instead to improve your mood and ease anxiety.
- If you wake up feeling sad you may turn to shopping. Try heading to the gym or choosing a fitness class instead of going to the shopping mall. Buying a new item releases endorphins temporarily and is detrimental to your pocket, however, working out releases endorphins and benefits your body. A home workout will also do in this case.
- Celebrating achievements is another moment where you tend to let your emotions control your spending. Instead of paying for everyone's dinner, take a day off to celebrate YOU. Indulge in self-caring practices you can easily do at home.

The above are tips you could use when you are about to indulge in emotional spending, but there are other ways you could avoid this altogether.

- Try to find the trigger that usually puts you off track. Try to find the emotions that trigger this and list them below:

_____

_____

_____

_____

Try the following tips to control emotional spending:

- If you find yourself about to go shopping because you are sad or feeling frustrated, take a step back and be alone for some time. Journal or chose to wait a week or so before making the purchase. If you do not feel like buying it in a few days it means you never needed it.

- Remove temptation. Uninstall shopping apps from your phone as those are the easiest to access when you are feeling tempted. Unsubscribe to the promotional newsletter. This will clear your inbox and keep you from emotional spending.

- Make alternative rewarding options a routine. Use self-care or regular physical activity to replace your emotional spending. These can reduce stress and anxiety, overall contributing to more controlled buying.

- Take exact cash if you are out running errands. Having a credit card readily available surely does not help.

- Make sure you schedule regular check-ups on your finances. Schedule these in your weekly planner and use this time to go over any pending bills, and credit card bills, and to check your account for any unnecessary expenses made during that week.

- Buy things you budgeted for. Before buying anything ask yourself whether your monthly budget includes this purchase. When setting a monthly budget be sure to include the necessities first, such as bills, mortgage repayments, groceries, and so on. If an appliance needs replacing like buying a new dishwasher, this should be included in your budget. Anything else should be either left to wait until next week only to realize you do not need it or for next month's budget if it is something you need to get at some point.

Although emotional spending is not a disorder, it can occasionally go too far and become one. A person with compulsive purchasing is said to have a psychiatric problem in which they are unable to control their urges and repeatedly and obsessively buy things they do not need. Compulsive shopping can have detrimental effects on a person's life and well-being, including issues with work possibly leading to financial ruin. Overall, focus on reducing stress levels and lessening your emotional reactions. Learn to self-analyze. This will help you feel less anxious, have better control over how you feel, and appreciate the things you have. All of this will contribute to less emotional spending.

Coping With ADHD-Related Challenges in Education and Career

Like kids in school, adult ADHD sufferers may have difficulties at work. They would occasionally have highly rewarding occupations. Others may have a range of difficulties, such as poor communication abilities, distractibility, procrastination, and trouble handling challenging projects.

While developing workplace solutions, adjustments, and adaptations, it is crucial to keep your situation in mind. Here are some tips for dealing with many of the ADHD-related limitations at school or work:

1- Distraction
   - Avoid multitasking.
   - Use empty office space, or silent areas in libraries, or ask if you can work from home when the office is full.
   - Put your phone on DND or direct phone calls to voicemail.
   - Keep a notebook to jot down ideas as soon as they come to you.

2- Impulsivity
   - Practice self-talk to handle impulsive actions.
   - Seek help from a professional like a coach to help you manage frustrating situations.
   - Request constructive criticism from trusted colleagues or classmates.
   - Incorporate meditation techniques regularly.
   - Take note of the situations that usually trigger impulsivity and find ways how to anticipate them, avoid and deal with them when they occur.

3- Hyperactivity

- Take regular breaks.
- Jot down notes during meetings to avoid getting distracted.
- Chose the stairs when possible and take regular walks,
- Prepare your lunches at the office or school and spend your lunch break walking in the vicinity.

4- Forgetfulness

- Take notes during lessons or meetings. Ask if you can record the lecture or meeting with the permission of the speaker.
- Break down big projects or assignments.
- Use reminders on your phone or laptop for deadlines or meetings.
- Use a diary or daily planner and carry it with you.
- Use sticky notes and leave them in visible places around you.

5- Boredom

- Use a timer when completing tasks.
- Take regular breaks.
- Break down difficult tasks into smaller steps.
- Choose duties or jobs with fewer routine tasks and more challenges to enhance brain stimulation.

6- Time Management
    - Assign a timeline for broken-down tasks.
    - Reward yourself when reaching deadlines.
    - Externalize time with alarms, clocks, or timers.
    - Set a reminder before every meeting or class.
    - Do not underestimate how long tasks will take you and avoid overpacking your days.

7- Procrastination
    - Choose working in a team or a group to feel the urge to do your part and contribute instead of putting the task off for too long.
    - If a deadline is not set, ask for one to be set.
    - Create a favorable environment before starting the task. Choose a playlist if you work better with music. Leave snacks and water close by.

8- Disorganization
    - Handle every piece of paper straight away, and discard or file it immediately.
    - If paperwork is an issue at work, see if an administrator can help with this instead
    - Use folders, files, and colorful dividers for filing to make it more fun.

CHAPTER 5:
BUILDING RESILIENCE

Resilience is the capacity to adjust to challenging circumstances. When stress, adversity, or trauma occurs, you still feel anger, sadness, and anguish, but if you are resilient both physically and psychologically, you could continue functioning.

Resilience – Its Role in ADHD

For many with ADHD, emotional dysregulation is a persistent and crippling experience. Emotional dysregulation symptoms, such as excessive rage, impatience, mood swings, powerful emotions, sensitivity, and more, are typical and sometimes highly upsetting aspects of ADHD. The severity of these emotional symptoms can be somewhat reduced by ADHD therapy, although traditional ADHD therapies do not assist with emotional balance as effectively as they do with inattention. Hence, learning how to develop emotional resilience is typically required for optimal results. Adults can use a variety of ways to control strong emotions and attain more emotional stability, from practicing coping mechanisms to attending to fundamental health requirements and seeking expert assistance.

Here are some tips for developing resilience despite your ADHD:

- Evaluate your routine and spot the bad habits. Poor diet and lack of exercise could be examples. Swap these bad habits for healthier ones and try this new schedule for 2 to 4 weeks.

- Examine your social circle and choose people who support and encourage you.

- Become aware of stressors and develop coping skills for them. If possible, avoid the stressors altogether like negative people. When avoidance is not possible, then coping with such a situation is key.
- Seek professional advice for childhood trauma and address it accordingly.
- Practice positive self-talk when faced with stressors.
- Shift your attention away from external stressors whenever possible.
- Try anticipating stressful situations if avoiding them is not possible, and develop coping mechanisms ahead of time.
- Turn to humor when possible.
- Try to be rational and change your perspective whenever possible.
- Seek counseling advice or therapy to develop resilience.

Developing a Growth Mindset and Positive Self-Talk

Many with ADHD have felt criticism for becoming distracted, acting impulsively, or missing an important meeting. All the negative criticism endured by your younger you at school and home has caused your mindset to switch to a negative one. You have been told you do things differently and are rarely praised for the good work. Switching your mindset takes some work but it can be done. Using your growth mentality frequently simply entails altering your self-talk. Instead of giving up, you devise a different strategy for dealing with the issue. You concentrate on how you can get better rather than allowing envy or emotions of inadequacy to dominate your thoughts.

Today, your worst critic might be yourself. Try to speak to yourself in a kind and encouraging manner. Speak to yourself with love and compassion, just as you would to someone else who has failed or made a mistake, rather than criticizing yourself. Being harsh with oneself is not always a terrible thing. You should critically evaluate your interpersonal abilities, but you should do it in a beneficial way rather than one that lessens your worth and value. Practice self-compassion by being kind to yourself. It is acceptable to recognize your failures because you are not the only one experiencing them and suffering is universal. Acknowledge negative experiences and learn the lesson.

Here are some ways you could practice self-compassion and positive self-talk:

- Turn to mindfulness when you catch yourself self-criticizing.
- Turn to someone you trust when you feel you are struggling.
- Keep yourself grounded instead of self-criticizing. Take some time to engage your senses and use an external natural timer to help you keep track of time as you do this. Light a scented candle or eat your favorite snack. Go for a walk.
- Have a reset routine prepared for these moments. Whether it is clearing your space, going out for walks, or meeting with a friend, once you bring your focus back, choose to start again. Do not make this a permanent trap. If there is something in your routine that does not work, amend it.
- To avoid failure altogether, understand expectations. When what is expected of you is unclear, ask; you cannot read minds. This applies in a relationship, at work, or school.

Embracing Your Strengths and Talents

The negative effects of ADHD have received a lot of attention. People with the disorder describe themselves as being more enthusiastic, creative, fearless, and resilient than persons without the condition. Even though there is still much to learn about the advantages of ADHD, focusing on them might help you cope with the disorder better.

Many people with ADHD experience low self-esteem and poor ego, sometimes as a result of years of receiving negative messages about their talents in comparison to people without ADHD.

Over time, these unfavorable attitudes can impair the quality of life and play a role in the emergence of mood disorders, anxiety, and other challenging mental conditions. Because of all of these factors, developing the ability to recognize your abilities is powerful and crucial to happiness.

If you were one to receive constant negative criticism as a young girl, you would find it hard to embrace the strengths that come along with ADHD, but here are some you probably overlook, but benefit you and those around you:

- You often have an open mind and honest conversations with those around you. You make your expectations clear, and this is beneficial in relationships and at work.
- Impulsiveness can become playfulness in a romantic relationship.
- Hyperfocus can be beneficial when doing the things, you love. This will lead to attention to detail and passion for the work you do.
- Because you do not mind taking risks, you are open to trying new things, others may be hesitant to do.
- Enhanced idea generation and creativity can be powerful characteristics for ADHD people at work and school.
- High energy levels can be positive, especially when engaging in activities that require it like sports competitions.
- You are more self-reliant and independent than neurotypical individuals. This can be particularly beneficial when you need to complete tasks or projects on your own.
- Being self-aware has people develop self-regulation approaches to control and handle emotions better. This is also beneficial when recognizing emotions in others and not just oneself.
- Your emotional hypersensitivity increases your intensity and sensitivity toward other people's emotions.

Exercise:

Here are ways you should employ to start finding your strengths more often rather than putting yourself down:

List at least five things that interest you:

_____

_____

_____

_____

_____

_____

_____

Look back at your life and list three successful episodes in your life:

_____

_____

_____

When do you feel appreciated the most? Describe one or two scenarios that happened:

_____

_____

_____

_____

List three successes you managed to complete in the past seven days:

_____

_____

_____

Realistic Goal-Setting With ADHD

With ADHD, goal-setting might seem unattainable. We can all struggle with prioritizing, breaking down work, and setting deadlines. The effects of executive functioning difficulties combined with time management, commencing tedious activities, planning, and prioritizing are some challenges of this condition. These are all crucial components of goal-setting and achievement, which might be more difficult for those with ADHD. Setting goals might help you develop and carry out a strategy that works for you rather than against you if you have ADHD. You have probably been told that creating goals is the most effective approach to achieving your objectives, whether they be to learn something new, complete a certain activity, or increase your level of accomplishment. Consider your strengths rather than the things that are making it difficult for you to carry out your ambitions. While certain ADHD symptoms may make things appear difficult, other symptoms may work to your advantage.

The relationship between task and reward may also seem different in neurodiverse individuals compared to neurotypical individuals. As a result, it is more challenging to design objectives and incentives in a way that supports the reward processes of ADHD.

The optimal goal-setting strategy for people with ADHD is frequently one that considers the difficulties with executive functioning. Calculating how long something will take might be more challenging if you have a problem with time blindness. Goals and subtasks must be written out as part of the process if working memory is a problem. It is crucial to constantly revisit your objectives over time to stay motivated and address any obstacles in your way to accomplishing them. Concentrating on how to work with your executive functioning difficulties to achieve your goals without feeling overwhelmed is helpful if you remain in an environment where you feel comfortable exploring, trying, and troubleshooting.

If distractibility is a problem, be aware that plans may change and strategies to accomplish a goal may change. However, if you maintain focus on your overall goal and comprehend how dopamine and time blindness may affect you, you can change how you accomplish the goal without losing interest in it altogether. Prioritizing urgent short-term goals is often the simplest for people with ADHD to complete. Long-term, multi-step goals might be quite difficult. One of the causes of this is that things that are "in the future" frequently do not feel as urgent and are hence less motivating. This is why setting targets and assigning deadlines for them may be just as crucial for ADHD smaller goals as it is for the main one. This will contribute to the overall goal and avoid you from procrastinating.

As an example, if you struggle with failing to remember tasks, you can write these down and keep them within sight. If you struggle with managing your time, externalize time and overestimate how long each task will take you. Allow enough time between tasks to avoid overpacking your day. If you struggle to start the task at hand, set the mood, clear your space, make yourself a nice coffee, or prepare a playlist for the time you find yourself struggling to start working on your goals.

Exercise:

The following is your ultimate goal-setting exercise. You can even use this for bigger or multiple tasks, to help you get started.

Find your priorities and write them below:

_____

_____

_____

List the things you are doing now that are taking away time from your priorities listed above:

_____

_____

_____

_____

What are your goals, based on the priorities listed above:

_____

_____

_____

_____

What are some of the ADHD characteristics you usually struggle with that might interfere with you reaching the goals listed above? Next to the struggle list ways you can overcome this.

Follow the below tips when working on setting your goals:

- Choose specific goals and use set measurable targets for them. Be realistic and choose achievable goals.
- Be sure to pick goals that are relevant to you. Having reasons why this goal matters to you will make it easier to achieve.
- Set a deadline for your goals and be sure to be realistic about this too.
- Evaluate your routine and make adjustments that work toward you achieving your goals. Use calendar reminders and alarms to help you stick to your goal-oriented routine.
- Include fun activities and rewards in your routine as you work toward your goals.
- Find someone you trust to keep you accountable.
- If you find yourself struggling to achieve your goals, re-evaluate your routine and find what is hindering your success. Make amendments as needed.
- Go back to the person you chose to keep you accountable and ask them for feedback or help if needed.

When you have ADHD, you can still achieve your goals. It all comes down to understanding who you are and what will work best for you. To determine what works best for you, some trial and error may be necessary. But unless you start defining targets, you will not know what will work. Do not try to modify or mend who you are while you are creating goals for yourself. Work with your strengths instead and make the necessary modifications for your deficiencies.

Helping Other Women With ADHD

"ADHD is just another word for fun, exciting and adventurous." — Julie Posey

For many women who discover they have ADHD as adults, the diagnosis is a relief. Suddenly everything makes sense... The need to constantly write yourself notes to remember things, the way disorganization seems to haunt you despite your best efforts, your difficulty remembering what the task that you were definitely going to do five minutes ago was...

Before you were able to view your experience through the ADHD lens, you probably felt isolated and misunderstood... And the tragedy is that there are thousands of women who feel this way – we are far from alone, yet we feel like we're the only ones 'failing' to handle life in the way we're expected to.

My intention in writing this book is to not only help you navigate the challenges you face, but to help you realize you're not alone – and you can help spread that message to more women like you... Don't worry, it requires nothing more than a few minutes of your time.

By leaving a review of this book, you'll show new readers that they're part of a large community of women with ADHD... and you'll point them in the direction of a resource that can really help them.

For many women who discover they have ADHD as adults, the diagnosis is a relief. Suddenly everything makes sense... The need to constantly write yourself notes to remember things, the way disorganization seems to haunt you despite your best efforts, your difficulty remembering what the task that you were definitely going to do five minutes ago was...

Before you were able to view your experience through the ADHD lens, you probably felt isolated and misunderstood... And the tragedy is that there are thousands of women who feel this way – we are far from alone, yet we feel like we're the only ones 'failing' to handle life in the way we're expected to.

My intention in writing this book is to not only help you navigate the challenges you face, but to help you realize you're not alone – and you can help spread that message to more women like you... Don't worry, it requires nothing more than a few minutes of your time.

By leaving a review of this book, you'll show new readers that they're part of a large community of women with ADHD... and you'll point them in the direction of a resource that can really help them.

Scan to leave a review !

CHAPTER 6:
BALANCING LIFE AND ADHD

To make life appear a little bit simpler, we need to embrace the truth that some of us are simply better at balancing things than others. A lot of people with ADHD have a variety of interests. It could be hard to follow all of those interests, pay the bills on time, and maintain daily responsibilities, all at the same time. Even worse, individuals closest to you might not be aware of the additional work required for you to perform many of the tasks they take for granted. Some people can juggle more things at once and are better jugglers than others. If you can juggle fewer things than some people, do not feel bad about it.

Finding Balance and Managing Burnout

If your ADHD is untreated, trying to balance your job, school, and other obligations can overwhelm you and lead to burnout. Burnout occurs when you no longer find enjoyment or interest in your regular activities when you view colleagues as adversaries who are adding to your workload, or when you disengage because you do not think it is viable to complete tasks. Burnout is exacerbated by ADHD characteristics such as disorganization, difficulty focusing, and poor time management. When you hyperfocus, your moments of being fascinated and absorbed in a topic or endeavor can last anywhere from hours to days.

You can start to overlook your needs, such as not eating adequately or sleeping well. This frequently worsens burnout.

Look out for the following signs of burnout:

- If you usually work out 5 times a week, you lack motivation and fail to keep this habit.
- You feel exhausted no matter how much you sleep.
- Your performance is poor as you find it hard to perform any task, no matter its importance.
- You may experience health issues like frequent headaches or stomach pains. This could easily be caused by the stress brought about by burnout.
- You become easily irritated and snap at others often.
- You find it hard to laugh or experience happiness.
- You become pessimistic and find it hard to see the positive in the things and people around you.

Here are some tips you can use to deal with burnout:

- Acknowledge that you are experiencing burnout instead of ignoring your present situation.
- Understand you have limits.
- Prioritize your tasks and choose the important ones. Focus on those and only if possible, turn to the less important ones.
- Do not be a people pleaser at your own expense. Learn to say no and refuse the things you know you do not want to do or have no time for.
- Taking a break is not a crime. Take a breather and do not feel guilty about it.
- If you think any aspect of your life needs fixing, acknowledge it and ask for help. This can mean seeing a therapist or a coach to help you with your skills.

Examine your everyday habits carefully. It is time to cultivate them if you do not already have them. The more structure you can include in your day, the easier and more effective time management will be. Take efforts to address any flaws that may be wasting your time, such as perfectionism or procrastination. Your hectic schedule could get lighter if you strive for simplicity. If you find yourself exhausted at the end of the day, you may need to look at wellness issues including sleep, exercise, and diet. Working smarter rather than harder could be the solution. Get support from your friends and loved ones. Instead of allowing their misunderstanding to contribute to the issue, include them in the solution. Above all, accept who you are and focus on your best qualities. Unless you are determined to make life difficult, it does not have to be.

Exercise:

What are the things you think cause burnout for you? List them below:

_____

_____

_____

_____

_____

_____

_____

Setting Boundaries and Taking Care of Oneself

Setting boundaries helps us look out for ourselves. When you know how to establish and uphold appropriate boundaries, you can prevent the resentment, disappointment, and anger that arise when boundaries are crossed. Boundaries might be anything from rigorous and rigid to hardly evident. A person with healthy boundaries is aware that being specific about expectations is beneficial because it determines both the conduct you would tolerate from others and the behavior that others could expect from you. If your boundaries are rigid, you could keep others at a distance or seem detached. You could also avoid close relationships or have few close ones. If you have no boundaries, you would typically struggle to say no, get involved with other people's issues, and overshare personal information. Creating healthy boundaries will mean you only share appropriate information with others, understand your needs and know how to communicate them to others. You would value your opinions and accept other people's opinions. Boundaries can be physical, sexual, emotional, financial, or intellectual.

When your emotional and psychological limits are violated, you must rely on your internal self which activates when boundaries are exceeded. Establishing limits serves far more purpose than only helping to define who you are. Your exposure to stress and the body's production of cortisol and adrenaline are both reduced when you have boundaries in place. Boundaries provide a feeling of independence. Also, studies have demonstrated a connection between loosened boundaries, particularly between work and home life, and unhealthy lifestyles, lower levels of enjoyment, as well as a higher chance of family conflict. You should thus keep yours under control.

Here are some ways you could do this:

- Use self-reflection to determine how and why boundaries are important to you. Think of the different aspects of your life and how these can be improved if you have boundaries in place.

- Choose boundaries you can start building slowly. Do so at a comfortable pace as long as you head in the right direction.

- Set boundaries from the very start. People will know exactly where they stand with you and you avoid having anyone cross your boundaries from the beginning.
- Be consistent with your boundaries and do not let anything slide. This will only lead to confusion and new expectations or demands you are not able to meet. This reinforces your beliefs and helps everyone remain in line.
- Incorporate boundaries into your routine. Choose to have some alone time once a week and be consistent and regular about this.
- If you feel like the boundaries you have in place are not enough, feel free to add more to these.
- Be careful how you use social media. Such platforms can overstep boundaries and enhance over-sharing.
- If you feel like someone is constantly overstepping your boundaries communicate this to them.
- Celebrate yourself and treat yourself with love and care. It is hard to set boundaries if you are your own biggest critic.

Boundaries are important, and it is feasible to maintain them without offending the people you care about, despite your concerns that doing so may make you appear unpleasant or hostile. Set limits without feeling bad about it. These are a type of self-care, and we deliberately want to include more of it in our everyday lives. Determining the boundaries that are most important to you and the best ways to enforce them may take some time and thought, but the work will be worth it in the long run for your mental health.

Finding New Interests to Improve Life Satisfaction

Whether it is reading, going outside, playing an instrument, or creating art, having a hobby is a fantastic way to pass the time and escape from your regular schedule. Your mental health and general well-being can be enhanced by investing time in a hobby or interest. According to research, those who schedule time for their hobbies are less likely to experience stress, depressive symptoms, and a bad mood. You may feel happier and more at ease after engaging in physical activities that have you moving about. Your interpersonal relationships and communication skills can be improved when participating in group activities like team sports. Your hobbies might be artistic, athletic, scholarly, or unique. You can decide on a hobby that you can do both by yourself and with other people.

It takes time and a deep understanding of oneself to control the symptoms of ADHD and discover things that are enjoyable for you. The following are some self-care ideas you could incorporate in your free time, to help recharge and unwind:

1- Physical Activity

Even a brief workout session has been shown to enhance motivation, brainpower, and energy because exercise releases chemicals that improve focus and attention. Exercise is sometimes compared to a dose of medicine because of the benefits it has in improving mental health. Zumba, martial arts, or HIIT are all excellent ideas for physical activities, especially if the gym may not be for you.

2- Listening to Audiobooks

Some ADHD individuals find that reading demands a significant amount of attention, time, and energy. Instead, listen to podcasts or audiobooks. By doing this, you may beat boredom and feel the pleasure and delight that stories can bring you without having to put too much effort or concentration into it. You may work on domestic chores or go for a walk while listening.

3- Brain Games

They can help you recharge your brain in only a few minutes, especially if you feel exhausted after a particularly dull and repetitive task. They range from crossword puzzles to sudoku. Brain activities may challenge and thrill your mind while simultaneously strengthening your attention and endurance abilities.

4- Meditation

Everyone can benefit from meditation since it develops the prefrontal cortex of the brain, but those with ADHD may find it more helpful than others. The prefrontal cortex enhances the brain's capacity for concentration, impulse control, and future planning, which for those with ADHD is sometimes a real struggle.

5- **Spend Time in Nature**

This activity is beneficial for any brain, not just ADHD ones. This can mean spending time outdoors even if it means spending time in your garden. This helps improve your focus and mood.

6- **Reduce Screen Time**

Staring at your phone or TV for prolonged periods can trigger sensory overload, a common symptom for ADHD individuals. The sounds, vibrations, and colors emitted by digital devices can cause this. To calm yourself, switch off these devices or simply put your phone down.

Incorporating activities in your routine will not only help you unwind but leave you more focused, and ready to face the challenges life throws at you, and overall increases your life satisfaction.

Exercise:

Choose two of the suggested interests mentioned above and briefly explain how you will incorporate them into your routine as form tomorrow:

Interest 1

_____

_____

_____

Interest 2

_____

_____

CHAPTER 7:
OVERCOMING PROCRASTINATION AND PERFECTIONISM

Procrastination is frequently exacerbated by some qualities of perfectionism. The most notable of these are perfectionistic concerns, which are primarily characterized by negative and critical self-evaluations, an excessive concern with other people's expectations, a lack of satisfaction from successful performance, an excessive fear of making mistakes, and doubts about one's abilities and actions, frequently in irrational ways. As they often result in bad effects on people's performance and well-being, these worries represent the more maladaptive side of perfectionism.

People rarely associate ADHD with perfectionism because of the stigmas around being lazy and disorganized. Yet it is a reality that is all too frequent for those with ADHD. What you want to do and what you can accomplish seem to be separated by a widening gap. The most prevalent cognitive distortion found in individuals with ADHD is perfectionism. It frequently shows up as procrastination or having a poor perception of oneself since the circumstances were not quite ideal. Growing up, ADHD symptoms can make kids the target of excessive criticism and punishment because of their disruptive hyperactivity as well as their memory and concentration problems, which can make it challenging to complete tasks like housework and homework. Also, studies reveal a significant link between perfectionism and impulsivity, another ADHD characteristic. Together, they create a negative feedback loop where an individual with ADHD sets unrealistic expectations, feels frustrated when they are not met, and then acts rashly out of anger. These choices may then have unfavorable outcomes that support the notion that they are worthless even more.

Procrastination and Perfectionism - Understanding Their Role in ADHD

You purchased the pocket planner. Your to-do list has been set up. You divided the duties into manageable tasks. You have set timers. You just stopped doing it after that, or you started doing it but got derailed. Perfectionism may become a problematic coping method. It is a method of attempting to precisely regulate every small aspect as if executive dysfunction could be overcome by simply working harder and being more disciplined. Perfectionism, as a coping strategy for ADHD, is problematic since it kind of succeeds. The strain and pressure you place on yourself to reach this unattainable level take the place of the dopamine reward pathway, a crucial source of motivation, not functioning.

The repeated negative feedback and self-criticism you receive when your ADHD brain falls short of your ideal level can ultimately lead to burnout and procrastination, even while the pressure to achieve can initially serve as a source of inspiration. Over time, this pressure not only increases your risk of abandoning your goals but also makes it hard to acknowledge your successes. It might seem like giving up on the only source of incentive you have to get anything done for perfectionists who have been using the stress-induced pressure to succeed as a substitute for motivation. Yet, you do not have to accept failure; you may still have the drive.

Finding effective methods to encourage yourself, control your ADHD, and overcome perfectionism is the target of the following tips:

- Shift your mindset from a negative to a positive one. Look at the things that went well rather than focusing on the negatives of the situation.
- Do not compare yourself to others. Try to be better than you were yesterday.
- Do not criticize others in the hope of finding the positive in yourself instead.

- Learn to accept praise. Not everyone is overwatching your every step to find your flaws. Learn to accept compliments.

- Go over the expectations you have of yourself. It is good to be ambitious, but it is not healthy to expect the impossible from yourself. It will only have you fixate on the little things, feeling disappointed, become stressed and overwhelmed, and worry too much. Choose realistic goals.

- Instead of overthinking your project and how unrealistic the conditions and deadlines are, focus on the small tasks you can do to achieve this goal. On a bad day, a project may seem impossible to complete but stick to doing the little doable tasks on these days.

Developing a Growth Mindset and Letting Go of Perfectionism

Talent may be cultivated, according to a growth mindset. This implies that it is all right if you do not know anything. You can learn and understand. A growth mentality also encourages embracing obstacles. It does not see the difficulty as a dead end. Instead, it is only a potential manner that they could need to shift course. A growth mentality also gains knowledge through criticism and feedback. They thus consider this input and utilize it for success rather than shutting down and blaming others. One of the few ways you can know if you are doing anything correctly is through feedback. Even when things do not go as planned, someone with a growth mindset perseveres, which means that they find a solution. Moreover, someone with a growth mindset will not blame others for mistakes that happen but rather take responsibility for it and learn. This can be you.

Here are the tips to follow if you want to develop a growth mindset:

- Appreciate who you are, without comparing yourself to others. Find value in the way you are.

- Practice mindfulness, whether through morning journaling, gratitude journaling, or a quick morning yoga session.

- Find your strengths and chose to build on those instead of dwelling on the thing you do not do so well.

- Practice positive self-talk. What is going on in your brain affects how you view yourself and perform during the day.
- Allow others to tell their opinions and do not be scared that yours will not be heard. You can reach a compromise. This is applicable at work, at home, and in relationships.
- Do not seek validation or approval from others.
- Find opportunities in every mistake you make. This is letting go of perfectionism and allowing yourself to grow.
- Change your definition of success. If you seek perfectionism, success needs to be redefined.
- Take ownership of your actions and character; the only things you have control over. Anything else falls outside your power, so taking ownership of the things you can control will help you understand that perfectionism is not achievable because you are not the only one doing everything, and not everything depends on you.
- Persevere. Believe that after falling you can get up, with more experience and better than before.
- Make sure your goals are clear and realistic. Set small goals using the resources and time you have.
- Act because when you do, your anxiety will quieten. It does not have to be the biggest step towards a goal you have set, but a small step will show your inner self that you are capable of succeeding. This step will take you closer to your goal.
- Evaluate your decisions and make sure they are not driven by fear. Think of the worst outcome if you do not succeed, and make sure you take calculated risks.
- If you are experiencing any blockers, do not hesitate to ask for help from a trusted friend or family member.

Pay attention to the things that make you happy and excited while keeping the source of your passion in mind. In what you do, how you do it, why you do it, and for whom you do it, you might discover passion, this is only if you go in with a growth mindset.

Practical Strategies for Overcoming Procrastination

Needlessly delaying choices or activities is known as procrastination. It is a widespread issue that can lead to a variety of problems, including lost opportunities and elevated stress. Choose the simplest action you can do to move closer to your objectives to stop procrastinating right away. Then, strive to take just that one tiny step while allowing yourself to make errors along the way.

This can be easier said than done for women with ADHD, so here are some strategies you can use to help you in the long run:

- Set very specific but realistic goals. Break these into smaller steps.

- Assess your procrastination patterns. Identify when, how, and why you procrastinate.

- Consider the negative consequences of your procrastination. Evaluating how this is affecting you and hindering your success will give you a boost to get started.

- With the previous tip in mind, develop a plan to reach your goals and avoid procrastination. As an example, if you always put off cleaning your home, because you always end up looking for your cleaning supplies, a sensible action plan would be to create a cleaning station with all the supplies organized.

- Follow through with the action plan, and if you fail at any point, take note so you can rethink your plan and do better next time.

- Allow yourself to fail at some point and do not put yourself down when this happens.

- Make tasks more enjoyable and easily achievable keeping in mind when and why you procrastinate so you can avoid this.

- Remove distractions.

- Set deadlines for your smaller steps toward your goals.

- Make a risk assessment plan and plan for the worst. Plan how you will handle these obstacles including your fears. Think of ways you can overcome these ahead of time.

- Choose ways you can increase your drive to perform the set tasks. Habit trackers and charts work well.

- Schedule reasonable breaks whilst you work towards tour goals.

- Put your time-management skills to practice when planning for your goals.

- Adopt starting rituals to get you in the mood to start instead of procrastinating.

- Choose either your easiest task if you do not feel like doing anything at all or your hardest one if your mood is high and you are feeling motivated. Allow yourself to switch from one task to another if you feel stuck with the first.

- Reflect on your past successes to help keep you motivated.

- Practice self-compassion as you would with a friend when you make mistakes.

- Allow yourself to take reasonable breaks you have already accounted for.

- Write things down. You will have a structure to follow and can strike things off when completed.

- Do not dwell on past procrastination. There is nothing you can do now. Focus on avoiding making the same mistake again.

Exercise:

Use this exercise as a reflection for the times you find yourself procrastinating. Think of when and how you do it. List how this impacts your life, that is; what are the consequences.

Ways you procrastinate	When does it happen?	Consequences	How can you overcome this?

Finally, keep in mind that doing even a little will be better for you than doing nothing at all because flawed action is usually preferable to taking none at all. Also, the longer you wait, the more probable it is that you will accomplish nothing. As a result, you should get started immediately while acknowledging that you will definitely make some mistakes at first but that you can eventually improve your strategy.

CHAPTER 8:
NAVIGATING THE WORKPLACE WITH ADHD

Many people spend the majority of their time away from home and at work. A person's work life is frequently essential for many of their social activities in addition to their salaries, professions, and growth. For many individuals, work may be challenging and complex. But those who have ADHD may encounter a variety of extra difficulties, and dealing with ADHD at work can be challenging.

Understanding the Impact of ADHD on Career Success

Individuals may struggle to carry out their necessary obligations. The following are some of the most common struggles faced at work by women with ADHD:

- Difficulty carrying out certain tasks effectively.
- Difficulty getting along with superiors and co-workers.
- Poor attendance record and tardiness.
- Difficulty learning new things.
- Their assessments and evaluations could be subpar.
- Struggle with office organization.
- Put off starting a new task or get easily distracted once at it, leading to too many projects going on at once.

- Get easily overwhelmed.
- May view administration and filing tasks as monotonous and tiresome.
- Difficult to follow instructions given if they are not written.
- Often known as unreliable and making thoughtless errors.
- Difficulty paying attention to what others are saying.
- Difficulty in maintaining levels of motivation in tedious work.
- Could come out as impolite or careless.
- Often underestimates the amount of time needed to complete any task, including arriving from home to the office on time.
- Often seen as daydreaming.
- Difficulty concentrating at work, especially if they function better at night, stay up late, and struggle to get ready on time in the morning.
- Overall showcasing a lack of confidence, self-doubt, and getting irritated by themselves or disheartened.
- If a workplace is not so tolerant or understanding of the struggles faced by ADHD women, they may get fired more frequently than non-ADHD women in the workplace, therefore leaving a bad record on their resume.
- To become successful and because of their ADHD, women are often required to work harder and longer hours, usually at a high personal cost.
- Prone to interrupt others during meetings and struggle to wait their turn.
- Take a while to make their point, speak too much, or dominate the conversation.
- Fidget, tap their legs, or play with their pen, often irritating others.
- Are often seen as workaholics as they struggle to relax and unwind.
- Could display aggressive behaviors toward others given their impatience and mood swings.
- Struggle to work in teams.

Navigating Accommodations in the Workplace With ADHD

Every woman with ADHD faces a unique set of difficulties. Hence, it is crucial to keep your situation in mind when you establish workplace solutions, accommodations, and adaptations.

Here are some tips for dealing with many of the ADHD-related symptoms or limitations at work:

- Request a private office or cubicle if a shared open space has you distracted during the day. If this is not possible use an unused conference room instead.
- Ask if working with headphones is permitted at work and do that.
- Request to work from home on some days or projects.
- Ask a receptionist or an administrator to take your phone calls as you work on important projects bound by deadlines.
- Keep a notebook handy to jot down any ideas as they come to you.
- Prepare for a meeting ahead of time by writing down any ideas you would like to share. This will let you focus on the meeting and avoid you butting in as others speak, fearing you forget what you have to say.
- Perform one thing at a time.
- Practice self-talk at work as well.
- Ask for feedback from your superiors and use that constructively.
- Use your lunch break to practice mindful meditation, or get out for a quick walk.
- Try to anticipate what triggers your impulsivity at work and develop techniques to avoid these or deal with them as they occur.
- Leave small tasks to serve you as a break when you are working on large projects. For example, leave filing or photocopying as your break from completing a task that requires your maximum attention. It will give you some time to move around.

- Tale notes during meetings to keep you focused and avoid distractibility. You can ask your superior to be the assigned person taking minutes. This will put your skills to good use and benefit you at the same time.
- Prepare healthy meals for lunch instead of buying food impulsively.
- If meetings are carried out online, ask for them to be recorded. If they take place in person, ask for the permission of the speaker and record them if they accept.
- Break down tasks into small checklists you can tick off later once completed. Set deadlines for each task to help you stay on time.
- Use reminders and alarms on your computer to help you stay on task and manage your time better.
- Use a daily planner for working days, and plan each day based on your duties and deadlines.
- Use sticky notes and leave them where you can easily view them.
- Choose a career that has motivating responsibilities.
- Reward yourself when completing big projects successfully.
- Set reminders for meetings ahead of time to avoid you forgetting about them.
- Do not over-commit or overschedule your day.
- For team projects, assign someone with good time management skills to manage this part of the tasks. They will help keep you on track.
- If you struggle with long projects, ask to be assigned shorter tasks you know you can perform well.
- Avoid leaving the paperwork to accumulate before filing. If this task can be delegated, do it.
- Keep only necessary office supplies and paperwork on your desk to avoid clutter, disorganization, and confusion.
- Use labels and colorful folders for filing, to make it easier to use, visible, and fun.

- Keep an eye out for nonverbal cues from co-workers, especially if some seem upset with you or your behavior. The quicker you discover there is an issue, the easier it will be for you to work on it and fix it. This will help not to tarnish your credibility at work.

- Create an optimal work environment depending on the projects you are working on at any given time. Need more office supplies, extra monitors, or a standing desk? Ask for them.

- When receiving instructions, avoid verbal ones, take notes, or request that an email is sent instead.

- Use your creative skills, problem-solving skills, and rapid decision-making skills to flourish at work instead of sticking to boring tasks.

- Practice proper communication skills and contribute to new idea generation.

- Use your open-mindedness and empathy to train new employees.

- Plan for each project you are assigned, including deadlines and resources needed to complete it on time.

- Find work-friendly fidget toys and keep them at your desk.

Building Self-Advocacy Skills and Seeking Support at Work

Your ability to advocate for yourself is essential to your success in all spheres of life, particularly in the workplace. Whether you are early in your career or far along the way, it is critical to make sure your voice is heard so you can highlight your successes and receive the support you require to strengthen any shortcomings. Being an advocate for oneself is crucial to your professional development.

Here are some tactics to get you started with self-advocacy if you want to make sure that your career is constantly moving in the right direction:

- Do a self-assessment and identify the value you bring to work. If you struggle with this on your own, take feedback from others. Once you find your weaknesses you know what training you require, and you can request that from your superiors. With your strengths, you know what new duties you can take on.

- Build a reputation for yourself. Make sure you deliver on your tasks so co-workers can also recognize your worth. Knowing you are capable but not being recognized by others will lead you nowhere.
- Without bragging too much, make sure your accomplishments are appreciated and valued. If you stay late at work to complete a task, or something cropped up and you were able to solve it on the spot, make sure your superiors know.
- Work on your team-player skills. Although the career you build for yourself is individual to you, you cannot succeed on your own.
- Your first job will present you with possibilities that are very different from those you will encounter later in your career; as a result, your self-advocacy techniques must shift. Your access to materials will increase as your career progresses. Make sure to take every chance to expand your network.
- Keep it professional and avoid letting your emotions or private life overlap with work.
- Avoid self-doubt and build confidence.
- Know what you are worth especially before asking for accommodations or a raise. Be prepared to list your responsibilities and the value you bring to the table if you are having this conversation.
- Work on building honest and genuine relationships at work without overlapping with your or your colleague's private life.
- Set a deadline for your outcome or career advancements. For example, work toward getting a promotion in 2 years depending on your workplace and career.
- When requesting any special accommodations, be sure to put yourself in your superior's shoes. Be prepared to discuss these and possibly go to them with a solution rather than just the problem. Understand where they are coming from ahead of time.

You should regularly use self-advocacy techniques including identifying your greatest assets and highlighting your contributions, being a trustworthy teammate, surrounding yourself with coaches, and building a strong support system. These measures will help establish your worth and enhance your career.

Finding a Career That Aligns With Your Strengths and Interests

Though it might be challenging, controlling your symptoms is not usually the hardest problem; rather, it is keeping interested in the job you are doing. Use the following exercise to find the job you will love:

Exercise:

List 3 topics you can talk about for hours:

_____

_____

_____

What is the one thing you would keep on doing even during the weekend? Think of things that usually excite you:

_____

_____

What are the things you consider boring and monotonous?

_____

_____

_____

Do you struggle with working in a team?

_____

_____

Do you see yourself being in charge?

_____

_____

_____

What are the small things that bother you?

_____

_____

_____

_____

Do you work well in a fast-paced environment?

_____

_____

_____

If choosing a job was not determined by the goal of creating a solid income, what would you choose to do?

_____

_____

_____

With the above replies in mind, take a look at your current job role and see how it aligns with your definition of an ideal job, and whether the things you are doing at present, fulfill your wishes. If you are still in college and soon off to join the employment world, this exercise will help you make the right choice.

Here are some jobs an ADHD brain would perform well in:

- Sales representative
- Owner of a small business or entrepreneur
- Food industry worker such as a chef
- Teacher or daycare worker
- Information technology technician or software developer
- Artist such as a painter or theatrical manager
- Engineer or architect
- Journalist, editor, or writer
- Healthcare worker such as a nurse or emergency first-responder

- Beauty therapist or hairstylist
- Sports people such as athletes or trainer
- Police officer
- Social worker
- Lawyer

Those with ADHD can succeed in the workforce. The secret is to perceive your ADHD features as benefits and look for careers or niches that make use of your particular skills. While picking a job, it is crucial to consider not just your ADHD traits but also your strongest personal traits, both the negative traits you can manage and those you cannot, as well as the things that grab your attention. After all, you are much more than just ADHD.

CHAPTER 9:
MANAGING RELATIONSHIPS AND SEXUALITY WITH ADHD

Understanding how ADHD affects your relationship is the first step toward transforming it. You can discover more effective methods of reacting if you can recognize how the symptoms of ADHD are impacting your relationships as a couple. It can be particularly challenging to retain objectivity and perspective when emotions are running high, as they frequently do while dealing with ADHD relationship concerns.

How Does Your ADHD Impact Your Intimate Relationship?

Here are some ways your ADHD could be impacting your intimate relationship with your partner:

- You struggle with being present now and later. Your partner may feel like they can connect with you now but have lost you a few hours later.

- You struggle to process sensory stimulation. The lights or sound around you can disturb you, as well as touch. You may enjoy this one time, or it could irritate you another time.

- You struggle to memorize significant dates, plans you have made with your partner, or tasks you committed to finishing.
- You have a short temper leading to outbursts and episodes of anger.

Sexual Health and ADHD

You may have been well aware of the way your ADHD characteristics are affecting your relationship with your partner because they often point out how you forgot about your anniversary, or to finish that house chore you both agreed on.

But what about intimacy? Sex is much like any other activity that might be difficult for someone with ADHD. During intercourse, you may find it difficult to focus, lose interest in what they're doing, or become distracted. It may be a struggle for your partner to point this out to you as you are intimate, so it is best for you to understand how your ADHD is affecting your sexual health.

Here are some ways your ADHD could be getting in between you and your intimate partner:

- Your lack of focus makes it difficult for you to enjoy physical sensations or sexual experiences overall. This can infuriate your partner, leaving you both unsatisfied.
- Being inattentive during sex can hurt the other party and interfere with the experience.
- Your distractibility could be leading to sexual dysfunction because you struggle to focus on the present moment.
- Your sex drive is too low. A person's sex drive decreases, and they frequently have no desire in engaging in sexual activities. ADHD itself may be to blame for this. Antidepressants, which are frequently used for persons with ADHD, might also cause this as a side effect.
- You engage in risky sexual behavior because of your impulsivity, like unprotected sex.
- Processing sensory stimulation during sex. Hypersensitivity may occur in people with ADHD. This implies that a sexual action that seems enjoyable to a partner who does not have ADHD may irritate or upset the person with ADHD. Someone with ADHD could find the smells, sensations, and tastes that frequently accompany sexual activity unattractive or irritating.

- Your hyperactivity is getting in the way. It could be quite challenging for a partner who has ADHD to unwind completely to be sexually motivated and this can upset your partner leaving you both unsatisfied.

Here are ways you can overcome all these struggles, overall improving your sexual experience with your partner:

- Boredom in the bedroom may be reduced by experimenting with various positions, settings, and approaches. Before sex, talk about ways to spice things up to make sure both parties are at ease and in agreeance.
- Explore how your sexual expression and intimacy may be impacted by your ADHD. They could take into account your needs. If they are aware that you are sensitive to light or strong odors, they could agree to turn off the lights and refrain from using lotions or fragrances.
- Do not be scared to ask a licensed sex therapist for assistance. Couples therapy and sex therapy are quite beneficial for many couples dealing with ADHD.
- Practice being present. Eliminate distractions and try soothing methods like yoga or meditation together. Set up dates and keep your word. Keeping this priority will prevent distractions.
- One of the greatest methods for someone with ADHD to assist their sex life is to take their prescribed ADHD medication regularly. These drugs can control distractibility, impulsivity, and hyperactive symptoms of ADHD. Nonetheless, a person should talk to their doctor about switching drugs if they see that their prescription is impairing their libido.
- It is also advantageous to keep the lines of communication open with a sexual partner. Partners may be better able to control their reactions and expectations if they are made aware of the potential effects of ADHD on sexuality. Building trust and closeness in a relationship also benefits from being honest with that person.
- Exercise regularly as it helps improve attention and minimize ADHD symptoms.

Practical Tips for Improving Intimacy and Sexual Health in Relationships With ADHD

How we take care of ourselves inside and outside may impact how we care for our partners as well. So, how can we employ healthy sex practices to facilitate more enjoyable sex?

Besides being healthy for your body, safer sex practices may also have a favorable effect on your emotions. By enhancing the pleasure and stress-free nature of sexual experiences, you are also promoting emotional well-being for you and your partner.

It is important to learn to set boundaries if needed. Be clear about the things you enjoy and what bothers you. Communication is important for you to maximize satisfaction for both parties and avoid unnecessary arguments. For sexual settings to be safer and more enjoyable, communication is crucial. It will all be more gratifying if you and your partner are upfront and honest with one another about risks, boundaries, and how to stay connected.

Speaking out about your concerns and comfort zones might help you feel less anxious and make sure you and your partner are on the same page no matter what happens. Even if your requirements don't align, at least they have been articulated so you can agree on how to move forward. Even when you are alone, consider what makes you feel attractive and confident. You may enjoy these things by yourself or with your partner, whether it is a silky robe, a decadent dish, or an erotic book.

All partners should be tested before engaging in sexual activity and discuss the results. This is a crucial step to ensure that everyone is aware of all concerns and can give informed permission. The decision to disclose your status and ask for your partners as well largely relies on you. Safer sex is one way to practice self-care. A fantastic strategy to increase closeness, safeguard your sexual health, and produce more delightful encounters is to take care of both you and your partners. Using barrier methods, disclosing STI test results, and seeking medical advice are some healthy sexual behaviors.

Everyone, including you, is entitled to a sexual life that is both healthy and enjoyable. Sex can boost your happiness, sleep, and endorphin levels.

CHAPTER 10:
EXECUTIVE FUNCTIONING AND ADHD

A combination of mental abilities known as executive function includes verbal and non-verbal working memory, adaptable thinking, emotional regulation, planning, self-motivation, and self-control.

Humans perform many actions automatically, such as breathing and moving out of the way of an oncoming car. Yet most of the other tasks rely on executive function. Executive function is used to some extent in each task or pursuit that calls for time management, decision-making, and information retrieval in the brain. A person may find it difficult to succeed in school, at work, or home, if their executive function is disrupted since so much of modern life, is process-driven and requires that people create and accomplish goals. Each day, we employ these abilities to study, work and navigate daily life.

Here are some of the ways these functions come into play daily:

- Working memory: Gathering information during a meeting so you can later utilize it for a presentation.

- Adaptable thinking: You have a calculation you need to work out and it has more than one possible answer.
- Self-control: You try controlling yourself to remain on task and ignore the distractions around the office as you work on a big project.

Focus, following instructions, and managing emotions are just a few of the difficulties that people with executive function issues may have.

Executive function is also referred to as the control system of the brain. That is because the abilities required allow us to make plans, establish objectives, and complete tasks. Executive function issues affect people's daily lives, both at home and at work. This set of functions is responsible for the following:

- Maintaining attention
- Planning, organizing, and prioritizing
- Initiating tasks and maintaining focus throughout
- Understanding the concept of different views
- Controlling emotions
- Monitoring oneself

Early childhood and the adolescent years are when executive function abilities often grow the quickest. Yet, they continue to grow into their mid-20s. Executive function issues are not diagnostic or a form of learning impairment. Nonetheless, it is typical of those who learn and think in different ways. Anyone who has ADHD struggles with it. Learning challenges may result from these issues, but they do not imply that individuals are dumb or unmotivated. Individuals with executive function issues are just as intelligent and diligent in their work as everyone else.

Here are some of the common struggles women with ADHD often face because of their executive dysfunction:

- They struggle to start working on that project, knowing it is due in a week.
- Despite having so much to do, they are unable to prioritize tasks effectively.
- Although being present in a meeting, they would forget what was just said.

- They struggle to follow instructions, directions, or steps.
- They are a creature of habit and often panic when a change in routine takes place.
- They struggle to switch their focus from one task to the other when the need arises.
- They fixate on things easily, even when the same things seem trivial for non-ADHD sufferers.
- They experience emotional dysregulation and seem overly emotional when compared to others.
- When thoughts come to mind, they struggle to organize or filter them. They often find themselves saying things they did not think through all that well.
- They often misplace or lose their personal belongings.
- They struggle with time management, often being late.

Strategies for Improving Executive Functioning

You know these situations all too well but have not yet managed to take control of them. Here are some tips and strategies on how you can conquer your executive dysfunction:

1. Practice Active Listening

   Whether it is a conversation with your partner, or friends or in a meeting, make sure you focus on what is being said, writing down notes and repeating what was said when possible. This keeps you engaged in the conversation, ensuring you do not miss out on important detail, and having a record of the conversation, especially for work-related meetings.

2. Remove Distractions Around You

   Clear your desk or maintain a decluttered space at home. If you need to work on an important project, choose to move away from the common office space into a quiet room.

3. Practice Mindfulness

   Before engaging in an important task, practice mindfulness. The controlled deep breathing techniques will help you stay focused.

4. Adapt Your Environment

   If you work better with music or prefer a stand-up desk, ask if these accommodations can be met. Adapt your environment to your needs and not the other way around.

5. Use Fidget Toys

   If you find yourself tapping your feet or playing with stationary, replace this with fidget toys. This can help you focus.

6. Do Not Let Big Tasks Overwhelm You

   Split them into smaller tasks, preparing for each one and sticking to the deadline you set for each of the tasks. This will help you look at a bigger project with less intimidation. Completing each task is another step towards the progress you are expected to make without overwhelm.

7. Make Use of External Reminders

   Set up reminders on your phone, smartwatch, or laptop. Use sticky notes at work and home for chores or reminders. Use visual aid like diagrams and charts to help you remember things. Are currently being trained for a new job post? Take your notes during training sessions and rewrite them using visual aids. This will help you retain information.

8. Choose an Accountability Buddy

   Choose someone you have a close relationship with and promote them as your accountability buddy. They will help keep you accountable for work projects, personal goals, and house chores if needs be.

9. Reward Yourself

   When you notice you have been consistent in your efforts, reward yourself.

10. Pomodoro Technique

    Train your mind to focus on each task for an hour or so and allow yourself a 5-minute break. Design a reward system that works for you. The Pomodoro technique is a great way you could use to help you focus for 25 minutes at a time for example, whilst allowing for frequent rewards.

11. Develop Routines

    Develop routines to help you with impulse control. Routines will help you remain consistent and get things done. Look at your schedule several times a day.

12. Have Everything Written Down

    Either ask for written instructions instead of verbal ones when possible. If your last meeting cannot be summarized in an email take the liberty to summarize it yourself. Keep a notebook with you and take notes.

13. Be Realistic

    When you need to move from one task to another or leave home for work, for example, make sure you allow enough time to do this. Be realistic and allow some buffering time for the unexpected. This will also help you to not over-plan your day.

14. Use Checklists

    Use checklists, either as part of your routine or write them down on sticky notes and stick them around where they will not go unseen.

15. Clean Your Space Weekly

    This refers to your desk and home.

16. Create Different Stations

    Have different stations for different tasks. This is especially practical at home when performing different chores.

17. Request Regular Meetings

    Meet regularly with your superiors if this will help you stay on track and keep you accountable.

18. Seek Advice From a Professional Coach if Needed

    Experienced professional coaches can provide ample support and can greatly enhance your performance. They can improve your professional skills such as communication, time management, decision-making, and negotiation.

19. Focus on Reducing Your Overall Stress Levels

    Spend more time in nature or with your pet, follow a mindfulness or yoga practice, maintain a routine, put items in the same place so you can locate them, and try to avoid or mitigate stressful situations. Furthermore, keep in mind that nobody is perfect, so try not to be too hard on yourself.

20. Train and Challenge Your Executive Functions

    Commit to doing something you enjoy that trains and challenges your executive functions, such as martial arts, playing an instrument, photography, dancing, or just gardening. Experiment with stepping outside of your comfort zone.

21. Declutter Your Mind With a Brain Dump

    Declutter not only your space but also your brain. A brain dump is just the act of emptying your entire mind onto a blank paper, much as how one could empty their wallet onto a table. You are letting anxieties, bothersome ideas, mental clutter, and irritations out. Just open a mental valve and allow all of those ideas to pour onto the piece of paper. Write until you can take a deep breath and feel your internal pressure ease.

Exercise:

Here are some of the things you could write down if you do not know where to start:

Errands to be done:

_____

_____

_____

_____

Grocery list and meal planning for the coming week:

_____

_____

_____

_____

_____

List 3 things you want to do during the weekend, as leisure activities:

_____

_____

_____

Work meetings for the coming days, date, time, and anything you need to prepare beforehand:

_____

_____

_____

_____

_____

_____

House chores that need to be done in the coming days:

_____

_____

_____

_____

_____

_____

_____

Any events coming this week, including venues, time, and anything else of note. For example, shopping for a bottle of wine to bring to a party:

_____

_____

_____

_____

22. Use the Eisenhower Matrix to Help Prioritize Your Tasks Effectively

The Eisenhower Matrix is a productivity, prioritizing, and time-management model that enables you to prioritize a list of activities or agenda items by first classifying them based on their relevance and level of urgency. It was founded by President Eisenhower. He utilized it to help him in setting priorities and address the numerous high-risk problems he encountered.

This method involves creating a four-box square with the axes Urgent and Not Urgent on the x-axis and Important and Not Important on the y-axis. After that, sort your list of items into one of the 4 boxes, with the Urgent-and-Important box positioned in the upper left necessitating that you take urgent action. You should have four empty boxes. This will enable you to sort the things on your to-do list into one of four categories:

a) Upper left-hand corner: urgent and important. The list in this box needs your immediate attention because the items here either have a deadline or need urgent action. Think of these duties as if your living room is on fire. The list here is very time-sensitive.

b) Upper right-hand corner: important, but not urgent. Although not super urgent, these tasks still need actioning despite it not being immediate action. You will need to schedule time for these later.

c) Lower left-hand corner: not Important, yet urgent. This list needs actioning but it is not super important. Typically, these things would be the ones you can assign to someone else to complete. Once delegating these duties your schedule is freed allowing for more time to be spent on something more important.

d) Lower right-hand corner: neither urgent nor important. The list here includes things that are not a necessity, and that you could go without doing. A typical example would be social media and scrolling through your phone. You can use the list here as rewards but do not allocate time for them during your day. Removing these tasks from the list will open your schedule, and make your to-do list less packed. Removing tasks from this box will help you avoid habits that inhibit your productivity.

You will be able to prioritize your days more strategically and successfully if you learn how to look at both your to-do lists and your list of long-term objectives through this perspective. Drawing an Eisenhower Matrix is a great place to start if you have a never-ending list of objectives and activities and you do not yet have a prioritizing framework to guide you in choosing which ones to focus on first. Here is a sample of the matrix to get you started:

Urgent and Important	Not Urgent, Important

Urgent, Not Important	Not Urgent, Not Important

23. Complete the Hardest Task First

    Another way you could prioritize work is by completing the biggest and most tedious task first.

24. Block Your Calendar

    Block your calendar to complete the tasks that need to be done first. Leaving chunks of the day to work on larger projects will help you focus longer on projects or tasks that need more time than other simpler tasks.

25. Rely on Consistency to Get Things Done

    Stick to your plan even if you do not feel like it, or if you think you can re-schedule or postpone what you had planned for the day, simply because you do not feel like it.

26. Try Mind Mapping

    Mind mapping is one of the most effective methods for visualizing one's thoughts. Mind maps can help you become more creative, recall more, and solve issues more efficiently than merely taking notes. While brainstorming is essential for most issue resolution, it is much more successful when done with mind maps. Mind maps are useful because they produce a visual landscape of thoughts that may be used to identify the root cause of an issue. When brainstorming, one might generate a plethora of ideas and thoughts, which can then be documented. A mind map can help you arrange your thoughts.

    A mind map, like a tree branch, is organized around a core thought. Concepts and sub-ideas related to the main idea sprout off from the core concept. Brainstorming using a mind map not only enables you to identify the problem and how it affects other areas, but it may also help you understand why the problem occurred in the first place.

    Mind mapping is particularly helpful in cases where you need to write long papers or memorize information while studying or learning something by heart. It is also helpful in cases where a project or idea needs to be broken down to be worked upon. While organizing and planning, mind mapping can be the best approach as well.

Although your ADHD has interfered with your executive functioning skills all your life, you have stumbled upon a source that can help you develop the skills you need to facilitate your life overall. Take the above tips and see which ones apply to you. Some methods may work better at home than at work and so on. Troubleshooting these strategies could be required, but you will surely find what will work best for you at home, at school, and at work.

CHAPTER 11:
STRESS MANAGEMENT AND EMOTIONAL REGULATION

Stress and emotional dysregulation can be two of the most common ADHD symptoms. If left untreated, these will highly interfere with your daily life. To better understand how these affect your life it is best to understand what they are and how they are displayed in your daily life when you have ADHD. This chapter will help you develop strategies to overcome their side effects.

Stress and ADHD

Many with ADHD experience impulsive triggers, forgetfulness, job loss, exam failure, or feelings of underperformance throughout their lives. Over time, such traumatic emotional events might make the brain think to always stay alert for danger.

Stress is the emotional and physical response to what we perceive to be challenging events. Finding specialists and adhering to a treatment plan might create worry and frustration, but it is not the main reason why ADHD sufferers experience stress. Most of the tension is brought on by trivial issues. It includes the cues people with ADHD hear all day long, including ones about their expectations of themselves.

Stress is exacerbated by situations like missed appointments, misplaced keys, and a sense of not having enough time. In addition, even when you know you are doing your best, you often feel like you could be doing more. The individual then receives unfavorable comments and rejection. It is a vicious circle. Frustration and impatience, two ADHD characteristics, may make stress and anxiety worse.

Cortisol, a hormone released when a person is under stress, is even found in higher quantities in persons with ADHD than in those without the disorder, according to researchers. The quantity of cortisol in their systems rose solely by thinking about stressful situations. Cortisol in excess is not healthy. It is intended to be created and applied immediately to keep us safe. Yet unlike wild animals, the pressures in our modern life do not strike quickly. The bad thing does not just happen and leave; it continues to worry us. It constantly bombards us in the news, on television, and social media. It is a persistent ailment.

Persistent stress worsens ADHD symptoms and potentially alters the chemical composition and physical structure of the brain, impairing cognitive function. The prefrontal cortex, which is also the region of the brain affected by ADHD, is impacted by stress too, according to researchers. Stress decreases neural firing and hinders cognition.

A person's capacity to organize information and activities, as well as to control their emotions, is frequently affected by a decline in their executive functioning abilities. We can observe certain impacts on the brain over time, particularly when stress is at a level that one might consider toxic, chronic, or traumatic. The ability to make decisions, create goals, and solve problems, are tasks we associate with cognitive self-regulation, and those would also be impaired. When stress and ADHD symptoms are present, interpersonal interactions can suffer, resulting in troubled friendships, marriages, and partnerships. The individual frequently finds themselves with a shorter temper and says things that are best left unsaid.

Managing Stress With ADHD

Here are some ways you can better manage your stress levels:

- Reframe the situation that caused you to stress and change the way you look at it. If your lack of motivation often causes you stress, it is beneficial to look at this ADHD characteristic trait as a way of dealing with a brain characteristic. If you do, you will be turning the flaw into a characteristic, reducing negative self-talk that is usually brought about by this characteristic if you view it as negative.

- Practice mindfulness, whether it is meditation or yoga, and try to make this a daily habit. Incorporate breathing techniques with this practice for maximum benefit.
- Get enough sleep.
- Practice physical activity regularly. Be it a walk or a session at the gym, schedule this in your routine.
- Incorporate fruits and vegetables into your diet. Avoid processed food and excessive sugar consumption. Minimize caffeine, simple carbohydrates, saturated fats, food preservatives, and alcohol as much as possible. Your daily habits should incorporate healthier omega-3 fatty acids, proteins, calcium, magnesium, zinc, and vitamins like B, C, and D.
- Do not over-commit.
- Use a calendar to plan your days and break down projects into smaller tasks to reduce overwhelm.
- Create a playlist of all the tracks you enjoy listening to. Use this whilst cleaning or walking.
- Keep a decluttered and organized space to avoid overwhelm. Deal with the paperwork as soon as you can.
- Choose small projects you think you will enjoy doing or try something new. From pottery classes to creating your first-ever travel journal, try embarking on small projects for leisure.
- Clear your social media feed and choose to see positive news both online and on TV.
- Try avoiding stressful situations in the first place.
- Work on your problem-solving skills and develop them.
- Work on improving your communication skills.
- Work on your time management skills. Use timers and alarms to help you do this. Start working on things or leave for your next appointment earlier than planned. Being late everywhere makes you look bad and adds to your stress levels.

- Control and manage your finances. Use technology to help you set automatic payments for bills and mortgages. Control your impulse buying habits.
- Learn to speak up for yourself and make your needs heard.
- Take control of your life by making ADHD-friendly choices, like choosing a career that utilizes your skills and appreciates your talents, instead of one that suppresses your true self.
- Do one thing at a time. Finish the task before you move on to the next one.
- Get support. Whether from friends, family members, romantic partners, ADHD support groups, or professional therapists, help and support for managing your ADHD and stress-related issues, can be very beneficial. You can voice your concerns and let others know about your struggles, picking skills and learning new ways to deal with them.
- Avoid overstimulating settings like loud places. If this is not possible, limit your time in such settings and mentally prepare for what is to come.
- Limit the time you spend watching TV or on your phone. You are more likely to move your body if you are not sitting down staring at a screen.
- Every week, take at least two days off to go out to lunch with your friends. If that is your thing, you could also spend the entire day playing video games.

Emotional Dysregulation and ADHD

The capacity to exercise control over one's emotional state is referred to as emotion regulation. It may include activities such as evaluating a difficult situation to minimize anger or anxiety, concealing obvious signals of grief or fear, or focusing on reasons to be cheerful or calm.

Every day, we are exposed to hundreds of emotional cues, most of which necessitate some action or response on our part. When being hit with so many stimuli every day, it is natural for the mind to become engrossed in some unpleasant thought or to unconsciously dismiss feelings. Emotional regulation functions as a regulator; it helps us sift the most crucial bits of information and drives us to attend to it in a way that wouldn't trigger tension.

A person with inadequate emotion control methods is more prone to succumb to mood extremes; their behaviors and behavioral patterns will always be dictated by their feelings. A well-regulated individual, on the other hand, will have greater balance and judgment of their moods and behaviors.

Emotional regulation enables us to make thoughtful decisions about which emotional consequences to embrace and which to ignore. Self-regulation is all about stopping between feelings and reactions; it urges us to take a breather before acting after objectively assessing a situation.

Value involvement is another important part of emotional regulation. When we respond impulsively without paying attention to what is going on within, we may depart from our basic principles and act in ways that are opposites to them. We develop the ability to keep calm under pressure and prevent ourselves from going against our essential principles through good regulation and self-control.

Emotional Regulation in Men Versus Women With ADHD

According to some research, men and women feel emotions differently, which may lead to distinct motivations for self-sabotage.

Females report higher difficulty with emotion management abilities than males, possibly because they experience both good and negative emotions more deeply. Females also report greater sad symptoms and have more trouble managing rumination behaviors than men. Females think about negative ideas more frequently than males and have difficulties thinking in healthy and positive ways.

The advantage of being more emotionally oriented is that, while women are more prone to rumination than males, they are also more prone to contemplation. Thus, they are more likely to comprehend and cope with emotions effectively.

Although men and women feel the same emotions, their internal sensations of intensity and techniques of controlling and expressing them may differ. One reason for this gap might be socialization, cultural norms, and learned habits.

Here are some of the most common moods and emotions experienced by women with ADHD:

- Changing from excited to unhappy, angry, or nervous in a few seconds.
- Alternating between difficulty paying attention and hyper-focus on a task.
- Experiencing spurts of energy and exhaustion throughout the day.
- Being easily distracted and abandoning duties.
- Often feeling annoyed or angry.
- Feelings of severe agitation and tiredness.
- Being unable to remain still or calmly wait without fidgeting or moving about.
- Interrupting others repeatedly but becoming irritated when interrupted.
- Being unconscious of the consequences of their words or acts in the present, but subsequently regretting them.
- Rushing through chores and making thoughtless errors causing them to be both irritated and demotivated.

The reasons for someone losing control of their emotions can vary. They may be inclined genetically to these quick alterations. They might not have witnessed or been taught appropriate emotional management abilities. They may lose control if they are reminded of terrible incidents from their past. Physical changes, such as tiredness, can also cause a person to lose control of their emotions.

Whatever the cause of our emotional volatility, the good news is that we can improve our self-regulation skills. We can all benefit from mastering emotional-control methods.

Strategies to Help Regulate Emotions

Here are some strategies you could use to help you regulate your emotions:

1- Become more self-aware. If you start feeling bad about something, try to give your emotion a more specific name, for example, are you feeling anxious, tired, disappointed, and so on?

How am I feeling at the moment?

_____
_____
_____
_____

What or who has caused me to feel like this?

_____
_____
_____
_____

How did I respond to this situation or emotion?

_____
_____
_____
_____

Could I name the way I am feeling in terms of emotions but in further detail? Examples could be disappointed, offended, upset, and so on.

_____

_____

_____

_____

_____

What would be a positive way I could view this situation as opposed to the negative way I am viewing it now?

_____

_____

_____

_____

_____

2- Practice mindful awareness if you are feeling like you are losing control of your emotions. This will help you relax and guide you toward making the right choices and taking the right actions.

3- Having a good night's sleep, eating a balanced diet, and exercising your body are all necessary for feeling satisfied in life. We have all seen how much better we may feel after a good night's sleep or after a nutritious meal. It might feel as if we have a completely new perspective on life, and it is much simpler to overlook minor irritations or upsets that would ordinarily irritate or disturb us.

4- Doing one thing that brings you happiness every day may lead to a sense of accomplishment and satisfaction. We may all benefit from paying greater attention to the good things that happen in our lives. Things that make us happy have been demonstrated to reduce negative emotions and promote good moods.

What are the things that make you happy? List them below:

_____

_____

_____

_____

_____

_____

_____

5- Cognitive reappraisal skills may involve strategies such as thought substitution or situational role reversals, in which we attempt to view a stressful event from a completely different angle. This can be something you go over with your therapists if you are following CBT sessions.

6- Establish your limits so that you may advise people to view your differences less negatively when you want them to. Letting others know when you need to move away from a situation that is making you overly emotional will benefit you and those around you.

7- Emotional dysregulation reduces our ability to adjust to life changes. We become more susceptible to diversions and lose our coping strategies, which is why we frequently begin to oppose progress.

Objective assessment is an excellent practice for developing adaptation. What would you have advised someone to do under these circumstances? If you wish, write down your responses and consider whether you are following the same processes for yourself. Take the advice you would give to a friend and follow it yourself.

8- Get used to creating your own rules or following your schedule. Consider carefully if it is essential in any given scenario to strive to act exactly as everyone else does. If not, develop your method to get the desired outcomes. This may assist in easing some of your tension and frustration.

9- Locate a secure online space where you can interact with others who can relate to your emotional needs. Get accustomed to banning and muting posts and pages that leave a negative impact on you or create unrealistic expectations.

10- Psychologists think that we all have the intrinsic ability to develop a broad emotional repertoire and divert our brain focus away from negativity. We can seek emotional support inside ourselves by practicing attentive self-awareness, or we can seek assistance from others by participating in constructive conversation. It is normal to seek help from a therapist or expert when our coping mechanisms fail; the goal is to build a healthy emotional shield that can channel our emotions and bring out the best in us. Positive emotions such as satisfaction, curiosity, and thankfulness are more restrained. Developing a habit of observing these pleasant moments might help you feel more resilient and happier.

11- Self-soothing by reminiscing about the good positive memories you had instead of the negative ones. This is especially helpful if emotional dysregulation is being brought about involving other people and the way they are making you feel. You can also self-soothe via music meditation and breathing exercises.

12- We can reach the mental equilibrium that we typically desire through emotional catharsis, which is a method of releasing suppressed emotions. You will need to name your feelings aloud, write them down, and talk about them with a friend, family member, or therapist without fear of being judged.

13- Stop. Take a deep breath. Decrease the interval between the trigger and the reaction. Listen to yourself and consider: where are you detecting sensations in your body? Is your stomach gripping? Is your heart pounding? Do you have pain in your neck or head? Your physical symptoms might provide insight into your emotional state. Inquiring about what is occurring to you physically might help divert your attention and relieve some of the intensity of the emotions.

14- Emotions are a natural element of how we react to events. Rather than beating yourself up for being furious or terrified, acknowledge that your emotions are genuine. Understand that emotions are a typical human reaction.

15- In the absence of proof, we fill in the blanks with our details. If you are feeling rejected because you have not heard from someone in a long time and assume it is because they no longer care about you, think of other possible reasons why this is happening. Maybe they are unwell, so do not just fill in the blanks with negative connotations.

16- Understand that you are in control of your responses. In most cases, we have a choice in how we respond. If you tend to react to emotions of anger by lashing out at people, you are probably aware of the detrimental impact it has on your relationships. You may also notice that it does not feel right. So, while it feels fantastic at the time, the repercussions are awful. Recognize that you can choose how you will respond the next time you feel angry or afraid. That acknowledgment is potent.

17- You do not have to keep placing yourself in situations that make you feel bad. As you start to feel intense emotions, start looking for patterns or elements that are present. Does something make you feel insignificant? Intense emotions frequently arise from our deep-seated anxieties, particularly those we conceal. What is going on around you, and how does it remind you of prior experiences? After you identify these triggers, you may begin to investigate why they are so significant and whether you might minimize their significance or their occurrence altogether.

Exercise:

Use the following exercise to help you identify common situations that cause you to lose control over your emotions.

A brief description of the situation:

_____
_____
_____
_____
_____
_____

What are the emotions you feel?

_____
_____
_____
_____
_____

What is your reaction to this type of situation?

_____

_____

_____

_____

How often does this happen?

_____

_____

_____

_____

Can the situation be avoided?

Y____   N____

18- Exercise self-compassion. Making time for ourselves every day is a terrific strategy to improve our emotional management abilities. Reminding ourselves of our abilities and attributes, as well as allowing our brains to settle in a flexible place, may drastically alter how we feel and react to our emotions. You can use relaxation or breathing techniques, meditate, or employ regular self-care routines. Gratitude journaling is also a great method to do this. Daily positive affirmations are also excellent for self-compassion.

Exercise:

Use the following as your gratitude journal starter. You can do this exercise either in the morning or evening, however, as part of your morning routine, this should encourage a positive mindset for the rest of the day.

Write three things you are grateful for:

_____

_____

_____

Choose one of the following positive affirmations and write it at the end of your gratitude journal for the day.

- I feel fueled and ready to face the day with whatever challenges it may hold. I will turn these into life lessons.
- I am worthy of love and care from those around me.
- I feel strong and confident today and always.
- I will live through the day without worrying about what could happen.
- I am more than the mistakes I have made in the past. Those are lessons that taught me to become a better person.
- I am where I am supposed to be and what is meant for me will find me.
- I will only try to change the things I can control.
- I am grateful for being granted another day.
- My present situation is the result of multiple factors from the past. I am in control of my future, and I can work on a better version of myself.
- I can get through these uncomfortable emotions.

These two activities can easily be done in the morning while you drink your hot lemon water or sip your tea. Evaluating the positives in your life at the beginning of the day will set the mood for what is to come.

Exercise:

Choose one of the following self-care acts and incorporate it into your day. Choose one which you know you can schedule and be realistic and considerate of the other things you have due on the day. Write it down in your journal and be sure to tick it off when done.

- A hot bath with bath bombs and candles.
- Book a relaxing massage.
- Prepare your favorite meal.
- Sit in your favorite coffee shop, people-watching or reading a book.
- Watch an episode from your favorite series.
- Take a walk out in nature.

There are clear risks to not effectively regulating emotions such as anger, worry, or fear. They include damage to relationships due to overreaction, unnecessary suffering, and missed chances that looked too difficult. Some strategies for controlling emotions, such as routinely bottling emotions up, may also be linked to decreased well-being and relationship satisfaction.

Emotional management is not a skill that some people have and others do not. That is a natural ability. In certain situations, we all handle our emotions well, while in others, we struggle. In human life, there is no all-or-nothing principle that governs emotional control. The way we understand our emotions determines how we respond to them. Emotional control does not imply being comfortable all of the time, nor does it promise that we will be protected from discomfort. We learn the ability to accept and control our emotions through emotional management.

Emotional regulation is all about moving forward and not allowing occasional setbacks to prevent us from accomplishing our goals. It is linked to ideals, expressiveness, self-compassion, thankfulness, and logical thought, which explains the inner calm that emotion management gives.

Regulating Your Emotions and Reducing Negative Thoughts With ADHD

At the end of the week, evaluate yourself by taking a positive approach.

Exercise:

List the ADHD strengths you have used in the past seven days. Examples would be open-mindedness, empathy, creativity, and problem-solving. List yours below:

_____

_____

_____

_____

What were the emotions you struggled most with these past seven days? Examples would typically be working memory, boredom, procrastination, and so on. List yours below:

_____

_____

_____

_____

Have you managed to reach the goals you have set for yourself this week? Y____ N_____

What were the goals that you have not managed this week and what can you do next week to reach them?

_____

_____

_____

_____

What emotions do you think have come in the way of you reaching your goals and going through with your weekly goal setting? List them below on one side. On the other side, list ways you could overcome them next time that happens. Keep in mind the list of strategies above to help you with this plan.

CHAPTER 12:
MANAGING ATTENTION AND FOCUS

Research indicates the neurotransmitters dopamine and norepinephrine may play a role in how your ADHD affects your attention and focus. The brains of people with this atypicality may have lower levels of these neurotransmitters than average people.

Norepinephrine mobilizes the brain and body for action. Dopamine gives you a little reward for action. Without enough mobilization and reward, many people find it difficult to start or finish many tasks. You most often find yourself struggling to avoid distractions or get back on task, stay organized, pay attention during meetings, remember things, and communicate with others. This usually results in missed deadlines, overlooked important details from conversations and meetings, or feeling undervalued at work or home.

Pharmaceuticals that alter brain chemistry can be beneficial. Yet many ADHD sufferers also discover that altering their settings and routines can help them focus more easily. Instead of battling your intellect, the goal is to use it. Most of us experience days where we struggle to focus. There are distractions everywhere. Setting high standards for oneself may result in you becoming side-tracked or giving up entirely. This lack of concentration can cause problems at home, at work, and at school. Even though you might not be able to make yourself concentrate, there are techniques you can do to keep your attention. Learning what works best for you will allow you to concentrate better. Not every technique will work well for your circumstance.

To find the ideal ones for you, some trial and error may be necessary. The following are tips and strategies aimed at helping you get started, stay on task, and avoid distractions.

Strategies to Improve Focus and Attention

1- Create a Routine That Gets You in Focus

   Start motivating yourself by choosing something that increases your dopamine levels. This could be making your favorite coffee or going out for one. Remove any distractions, like clutter around you or notifications on your phone. List down the tasks you need to do and any steps for each. Set the mood for your focus to kick in and remain there. Choose your favorite music and start working on the task planned. Keep food and snacks close by to avoid getting distracted.

2- Be Flexible With Your Focus Routine

   Look back at what worked with this routine and identify the struggles you encountered. The question is whether the activities you chose were enough to increase your dopamine levels, or if you eliminated all possible distractions. Identify what did not go so well and how you could change this next time.

3- Use the Zeigarnik Effect

   According to the Zeigarnik Effect, incomplete chores are more difficult to forget than those that have not even been started. This implies that starting a project will make it tougher for your brain to forget or disregard it, even if you only work on it for 10 minutes. Set a timer for 10 minutes and work on the job throughout that time. Once you have started, the enormous job will become an incomplete chore, causing your mind to focus on it and come up with a solution.

4- Write a To-Do List

   Every morning list down the things you need to do that day. This is not a goal-setting list or a list you could complete during the week, but rather, it is a list you must abide by during the day and the things listed here should be completed by the end of the day. Be realistic and list about two major things and two to three less important priorities that still need to be completed by the end of the day.

5- **Respect Your ADHD**

Honor your intellect. Just as crucial as knowing when your mind is clear and you can focus and pay attention to duties, is knowing when you are not in the zone. Permit yourself to switch to easier chores when you are completely out of it. Long term, more will get done.

6- **Try to Overcome Your Perfectionism Traits**

Do not expect your perfectionist tendencies to vanish overnight; instead, expect to lessen your worry, boost your self-esteem, and increase your productivity along the road. Keep an eye out for your tendencies and try to focus on the positive side of things. Allow yourself to make mistakes and be realistic with your goals. Welcome criticism and use it to grow and learn. Minimize the pressure you put on yourself. Avoid negative influences and shift your focus on finding meaning in what you do rather than seeking perfection.

7- **Set Deadlines for Projects Even if They Do Not Come With One**

Some tasks come with a deadline especially if they are work or school projects. If tasks do not have an official deadline, create one for yourself. If a big project came with one final deadline, when breaking it down into smaller tasks set deadlines for each one.

8- **Use Your Tools**

You can keep your attention throughout the day by using electronic alarms, reminders, and scheduling tools. These apps can be configured to alert you to pending commitments or to nudge you repeatedly to complete time-sensitive chores.

9- **Break Big Projects Down**

Breaking down a challenging activity into smaller objectives could be helpful. Little objectives inside a bigger objective might keep a project from seeming to be taking too long. Little objectives may also keep you feeling accomplished, which could keep you motivated.

10- Have a Relaxation Technique of Your Choice

Incorporating relaxation sessions when you require a rapid focus method could be the answer. You may refocus your thoughts by using relaxation techniques that you can apply, such as deep breathing exercises or meditation.

11- Make Physical Activity Regular

Exercise increases oxygen to the brain and stimulates hormone release. These all help with focus in the long run.

12- Know When to Stop

If you have been working on a project for hours and feel like you cannot take it anymore, be realistic and allow yourself a break or stop completely and reschedule for another day. There is so much focus you can use, and you need to know when it is all used up, or when your medication has simply worn off.

13- Do Not Beat Yourself Down

Self-criticism will not help because it is difficult to focus on a task. Working nonstop is challenging. A small bit of kindness can go a long way toward preventing you from giving up too quickly. Be tolerant of yourself. Your efforts are commendable. It is crucial that you avoid letting your level of productivity determine your value, regardless of whether you are or are not productive. If you do fifteen things today or nothing at all, you are still valuable. Do not be afraid to contact a specialist for help if maintaining focus becomes too difficult.

14- Work on One Thing at a Time

Contrary to popular belief, evidence shows that persons with ADHD are less effective at multitasking than normal people. To cease multitasking and instead make it as simple as possible to concentrate solely on one job at a time is one way to help become more focused.

Tips to Help Reduce Distractions

1- Place the Less Important Things in the Parking Lot

   Keep a notebook with you all the time and when things come to mind, write them down. These things will eventually get placed on your daily to-do list but for the time being, they are not so important. Creating a parking lot with these things will help you not to forget them but keep you focused on the more important tasks.

2- Know What Overwhelms You

   By recognizing the factors that make you feel overwhelmed, you can end this cycle. Gaining control over your overwhelm will not stop it from happening every time, but you will be better able to predict it and make plans in advance. For some, it is getting hungry for example. Being prepared for this means you will have snacks on hand.

3- Minimize Distractions

   Sometimes closing the door to your room or office and putting your noise-canceling headphones on is all you need to get started.

4- Dismiss Negative Thoughts

   Be aware of your typical thinking patterns and schedule a time to give them the attention they require, no more no less.

5- Schedule Breaks

   While project interruptions might put you at risk for distractions, setting an alarm for brief pauses may encourage you to return to what you were working on.

6- Keep a Clean Space

   Thoughts are not the only type of distraction. Distractions might result from sitting in an untidy environment. In the middle of drafting an email, you could find yourself wishing to rearrange your space. You can avoid being distracted if you maintain your workspace neat and organized.

7- **Put Your Phone Away**

With the ease with which social media and gaming are accessible on smartphones, it is simple to spend hours video viewing and meme posting. Even if you succumb to the need to pick up your phone, shutting it off completely will help you resist the urge to browse the internet.

8- **Narrow the Things in Front of You**

While working on a particular task, keep visible only the things related to your project.

Techniques to Help You Stay on Task

1- **Use the "Eat the Frog Theory"**

This simply means finding your biggest task and completing even the simplest of duties related to it. This does not mean putting the whole task on the list and completing it at once, but rather getting started on it. This will avoid procrastination, and often it is what you need to get started.

2- **Not All Distractions Are Bad**

Consider exercise. While taking a break from work to go for a walk could seem like procrastination, doing so really strengthens the brain and can make you more productive when you return. Choose the "positive distractions" that suit you best. Effective examples include meditation, a little dancing break, or a thoughtful art project. Set a timer and adhere to it if you are concerned that you will get lost in your distraction.

3- **Appoint Someone to Hold You Accountable**

Accountability sharpens attention and, in the long run, brings about change. Having a support system might help you stay on track throughout the day. Someone else can help you be responsible for your actions, whether at work or home. If you appear to be preoccupied, they can help you by gently guiding you to focus your energies. If you are unable to have a reliable support person nearby, having someone call you frequently during the day could help.

4- Schedule Time for Planning

One of the biggest focus killers is poor preparation; it is difficult to stay in the zone when you do not know what you are meant to be doing. You should schedule frequent, brief planning meetings to outline priorities and deadlines for the future days or weeks. Of course, nothing is definite; circumstances might change, and crises may occur. Yet even if you get side-tracked, having a broad understanding of your objectives and how to prepare to attain them helps you regain focus. Making a plan helps you stay focused on your goals and develop a timeframe so that you can stay on schedule.

5- Make Sure Your Goals Are Identified and Set

Understanding what is expected of you can help you avoid distractions and have a positive attitude. The clearer you are, the simpler it is to focus and complete tasks. Asking yourself these questions might help you focus on a project if you are having problems doing so: What do you want to achieve, what are the expectations for this project and from myself, are you understanding what needs to be done?

How motivated you are to accomplish a work depends on how well you understand it. Vague projects and tasks sometimes seem too overwhelming to start, or you might not know where to start. Outlining what has to be done might be made simpler the more specifics you are aware of.

6- Use Fidget Toys

Stress balls, fidget spinners, and even chewing gum can occasionally provide your brain with a healthy release that does not divert you from your main objective.

7- Use the Pomodoro Technique

Francesco Cirillo, an Italian business student, was trying to figure out how to accomplish more in a day in the late 1980s. He once tried using a kitchen timer to divide his tasks into five-minute breaks and 25-minute work sessions. He would take a lengthier rest of 30 minutes after three rounds. He found that using this technique helped him focus and study more. He gave his method the term "Pomodoro" after the kitchen timer. Use a physical timer or any app on your phone to help you maintain your focus for 20 or 30 minutes. Schedule a 5-to-10-minute break for every block of time you manage to focus.

8- **Switch Tasks When You Start Losing Focus**

Switch to another task to constructively put off finishing one when you feel bored. Instead of attempting to drive yourself through one job, you might discover that playing between two or three of them works better.

9- **Block Your Calendar**

Plan what you should be working on ahead of time, keeping in mind priority tasks that are due. Block your calendar for each task and set reminders either on your phone or laptop calendar to help you remember. Stick to the schedule. By allowing you to decide in advance, whether it be weekly or daily, what you should work on and what can wait or be transferred to someone else, it helps you get organized. Setting aside time to work on one task and one task only also helps you avoid distraction. Pay attention to your energy flows for time blocking. Schedule your most mentally demanding activities for the afternoons and your mindless ones for the mornings if you can hyperfocus better then.

Exercise:

Try this exercise to help track your focus throughout the day.

When do I focus best during the day? Is it in the morning or late at night? Will it help if I started the day earlier, or do I work better in the evening when everyone has either left the office or retrieved to their beds at home?

_____

_____

What are the things I do at present that help motivate me to start working on any task?

_____

_____

What helps me maintain my focus when I am working on a task? Examples could be music, fidget toys, snacks, and so on. Keep the things you list below in mind for the next time you want to maintain your focus.

_____

_____

_____

_____

What would help you recharge during a break but not fully distract you from the task at hand? Examples would be taking a 10-minute break to dance to your favorite tunes, taking a walk outside, playing your favorite video game, preparing your favorite snack, calling a friend, and so on. Keep the things you list below in mind for the next time you have a break scheduled as you work on your task.

_____

_____

_____

_____

Focusing poorly does not reflect well on you or your work ethic. Even though it may be difficult to maintain attention during tedious chores, there are techniques you may use to do so. Focus cannot be forced, but the right physical and mental conditions can help it flourish. Combining the elements that enable your attention to thrive and working with it rather than against your ADHD brain are the answers.

CHAPTER 13:
BUILDING HEALTHY HABITS AND ROUTINES

Add structure to your life if you want to have a productive day. Otherwise, you will fly around life forgetting things, ignoring things, and putting things off. Easier said than done right? Structure makes things run more smoothly and maintains order.

We often deal with feeling overloaded or that time is running out when we have ADHD. Researchers agree that routines that offer structure and take into consideration the behaviors of individuals with ADHD might be beneficial. Routines assist us in creating healthy habits to deal with executive functioning issues, whether it is getting out of bed in the morning, concentrating on tedious work, or winding down before bedtime. Working memory, time blindness, and issues with transition times are just a few of the executive functioning difficulties that are typically associated with ADHD.

According to research, creating routines can be a fantastic approach to reducing stress and increasing control over daily chores. Because the only systems we have been taught have been optimized for neurotypical people, ADHD adults frequently detest structure and regularity. Adults with ADHD and neurotypical people might have extremely diverse worldviews. Hence, it is important to create a routine that works for your neurodiverse brain. Because of these variations, the behaviors ADHD adults engage in must be tailored to their needs. Otherwise, a routine might feel useless.

A supportive framework for ADHD adults may be created by designing a daily schedule that is optimized for time blindness and working memory issues and contains enough stimulating activities to support dopamine dysregulation. One of the challenges ADHD individuals might face is forming a habit that seems to work but then rapidly giving it up and reverting to old behaviors. One of the reasons we sometimes come out as inconsistent is because of this beginning and stopping.

Maintaining routines is important if you want to feel content and productive in your life. They can enhance mental wellness and lessen stress and anxiety. We act according to our habits. These automatic reactions are made up of repeated loops. The components of habit loops include signals, recurrent behaviors, and reinforcer rewards. Habits are patterns of conduct that are repeatedly used to the point that they are virtually automatic.

Tips for Creating and Maintaining Healthy Habits

Below are some tips to help you create and maintain healthy habits:

- Sit down and write a daily schedule ahead of time.
- Schedule tedious tasks first thing in the morning when your attention is set to be higher. Leave simpler tasks for the afternoon or evening when you are more likely to have low energy and focus levels.
- Schedule more time than you think for every task you have.
- Keep your schedule visible, written down, and where you can easily see it.
- Break bigger projects or tasks into smaller ones.
- Cross off tasks once completed. This small but valuable step will help you gain a sense of accomplishment.
- Do not strive for perfection when creating your schedule. Keep things as simple as possible.
- Use timers and reminders on your smartwatch or phone to help you stay on track with your schedule.

- Consider what are the things that help you stay focused and motivated. For example, if a clean kitchen or an empty laundry basket minimizes your distractions, make sure you schedule time for this before you start working on that work presentation or that school assignment.

- Be consistent. Frequently sticking to your planned schedule will help you create healthy habits. Over time, you will need less and less motivation to start the tasks, as they become engraved in your daily routine.

- Keep a separate leisure and work environment. If you work from home, make sure to work from a designated desk area and not in bed. If you work from the office, be sure to stand up during your lunch break and have your lunch in the canteen or outside the office premises. This will reduce your stress and anxiety during your leisure and help with productivity during working hours.

- Make sure you schedule time for yourself. Rest and socialization are as important as work. This includes leaving adequate time for sleep.

- Be kind to yourself if you fall off your schedule. This can happen once in a while, but if you find yourself rarely sticking to your schedule, consider changing the schedule itself, as it is probably not working well for your needs.

- Give yourself the credit you deserve when you complete the things on your to-do list, stick to your schedule, or even stick to your daily meal plan.

- Allow 2 weeks of trying the same schedule before giving up and saying it is not working out for you.

- Choose one small thing and schedule it every day. Choose that one thing you know will help you feel more accomplished and productive. For example, this could be making your bed first thing in the morning or going to the gym.

Creating an ADHD-Friendly Morning Routine

Creating and sticking to a morning routine can help manage some of your strong ADHD symptoms. Between your habit of getting sidetracked in the morning and that sluggish feeling when you wake up, having a morning routine to follow could be the solution. You have been struggling with leaving the house on time in the morning and cannot stop yourself from doing everything except getting ready for work.

Use the following tips to help design your ADHD-friendly morning routine:

- Wake up as soon as your alarm goes off or a little while after but do not procrastinate.
- Put on music as you get out of bed or start your favorite podcast. Move to a different room in the house.
- Do not spend your morning scrolling on social media or checking your emails, especially not while still in bed.
- If you are one to make yourself a hot beverage or breakfast now is the time. Choose a healthy breakfast that will keep you fuller for longer. This will help you remain focused on the task at hand rather than constantly looking for snacks.
- Schedule ten minutes for yoga or meditation. If you feel like you work out better in the morning, schedule this into your morning routine.
- Look at your calendar and check what appointments, or deadlines you have due for the day.
- If you work better with daily planners rather than weekly, take time during breakfast to schedule the day ahead.
- Get ready and change into something other than your PJs, even if you have nothing planned for the day or you are working from home.
- If you need to leave the house, grab whatever you need, like keys, headphones, phone, and so on, and do not let anything distract you from leaving your house on time.

Creating an ADHD-Friendly Evening Routine

Use the following tips when designing your evening routine:

- Set a bedtime alarm to remind you to start getting ready for bed. This means you will stop working or switch off the TV if you are still doing that.
- Incorporate some relaxation activities, like a hot bath or a few minutes of reading.
- Plan to sleep at least seven to eight hours, this is not negotiable.

- Prepare things you know you will need the next day to help you get ready quicker in the morning.
- Take some time to reflect on the day you had. Tick off any tasks you managed to complete and reschedule the ones you did not manage for the coming days.
- Reflect on your emotions during the day and write how you felt.

Having a schedule does not imply that you will or can always adhere to it. Life happens, and situations in life do not necessarily follow a predictable pattern. Having a routine, on the other hand, helps you get back on track faster and rediscover your concentration quicker.

Designing a Personalized Daily Routine

Right now, ask yourself if your daily routine is supporting you. If the response is "no," it is time for a change.

How to Get Started?

Remembering to approach the process of constructing the routine as a tedious chore that needs dopamine is the secret to developing an efficient routine for adults with ADHD. Take yourself out on a date, maybe to a coffee shop, or turn on your favorite music to reinforce this good behavior change. Once you are in a stimulating setting, you may start planning and organizing your daily schedule. You may achieve this by exploring and then troubleshooting.

How to Personalize It?

Create a strategy based on your objectives. Changes should be made depending on what worked and whatever executive functioning issues you discovered negatively impacted your behavior after testing your routine for a week. This might be as easy as writing a message on your bedroom door that you can read as you leave the room while you are initially developing a routine. But it might be beneficial to incorporate them into your calendar as you develop additional habits.

Exercise:

Identify one thing about your day that you do not like. Be detailed, yet keep your attention limited. What you want to modify is this.

_____

_____

_____

_____

Set up the procedures required for your new routine. Make a huge list of everything that has to change for you to recreate your routine.

_____

_____

_____

_____

_____

_____

_____

Based on the relevance or urgency of the activities, create a shorter list of only three items from this lengthy list.

_____
_____
_____
_____
_____

Next, divide each of these components into shorter portions. By altering one aspect of an issue at a time, you want to set yourself up for success. Be sure to include the kinds of supplies or help you will require. Keep your aspirations low; trying to change too much too fast typically backfires.

_____
_____
_____
_____
_____
_____
_____

Determine what drives you. Is it anything outside of you, such as a great cup of coffee, praise from your boss, or no late penalties on your credit cards? Or is it an internal factor, such as achieving a personal objective or enjoying the gratification of the achievement itself?

_____

_____

_____

_____

_____

_____

_____

Think about how you will feel if you do not stick to the new routine you have established for yourself. Think about how you want to perceive the present and your desired future.

_____

_____

_____

_____

_____

_____

_____

After you have determined which habits you want to change, create a detailed strategy and enlist the help of accountability partners. They will support you when you run into difficulties and will compassionately and firmly help you stay to your stated aim. An intention becomes a plan of action when it is shared in public. Whom will you assign as your accountability partner?

_____

_____

_____

_____

_____

_____

_____

_____

_____

Starting a new routine as an adult with ADHD might bring up regrets from the past. Yet, with basic support for ADHD in place, we can frequently proceed toward creating long-lasting, reliable routines that aid in lowering that sense of everyday overload.

These routines, whether for the morning, sleep, exercise, cleaning, self-care, or meals, provide the framework that helps establish the order that we all need to get by. You may create new habits that will help you feel less stressed and anxious every day with practice.

CHAPTER 14:
PROFESSIONAL HELP AND SUPPORT

Adult ADHD treatment techniques that are comprehensive are those that include multiple distinct, complimentary treatments to minimize symptoms. This perfect mix may include medicine, diet, exercise, and behavioral treatment for one person. For others, it may entail taking vitamins, practicing CBT, and attending an ADHD support group.

Identifying and managing the proper treatments involves study, preparation, organization, and perseverance. Discuss your alternatives with your doctor. If you use a medicine, ask your doctor about his or her experience with complementary therapy choices. If you do not want to take medicine, choose a specialist in the therapies you wish to employ; a nutritionist or a psychologist who specializes in behavior therapy, for example.

Finding the Right Treatment That Works for You

Medication, while generally helpful, is not a simple solution. Before beginning pharmacological therapy, patients should consider that it might take months to find the correct drug, dose, and regimen.

For certain people, every drug has adverse effects. It is a trial-and-error procedure. It will take some time for you to find the most suitable drug and dose with the fewest or no adverse effects. To get the most out of your medicine, you must speak with your doctor and listen to their advice, especially during the early treatment phase. This communication is required to change the dose and control side effects on time.

Because adult ADHD is a newer specialty, many clinicians have not had formal training as part of their education. It is the responsibility of each professional to stay current on ADHD issues by attending seminars or workshops and reading professional publications and books on the subject. Some professionals are more interested in and experienced in this field than others. Some people refuse to accept ADHD as a real disorder. Many of us are so amazed by doctors that we find it difficult to raise questions, especially if we have doubts about their competence. Will this sound impolite? Will the doctor get offended? It is your right to know the qualifications of any professional with whom you may be dealing, and most doctors are aware of this.

Inquire about specialists in your region who may be able to assist you. There are some questions you can ask to help you choose the best healthcare professional to help you with managing your ADHD. Often, the desk clerk can provide you with the answers and the information you require to make an educated decision.

1. How many adult ADHD patients have you seen?
2. How long have you been dealing with ADHD in adults?
3. What steps are included in your evaluation and treatment process? Written exams or interviews? Do you look into the patient's family history? Behavior changes? Medication?
4. What are the expenses?
5. Have you completed any specialized training in adult ADHD diagnosis or treatment?
6. What kind of insurance does this office accept?
7. Are online visits possible (if you live a long distance away from the clinic, this would be helpful)?
8. Is this clinic equipped with adjunct services such as psychotherapists, social workers, coaches, educational specialists, dietitians, and care coordinators? If not, do you have any recommendations?

Psychiatrists are the professionals we should expect to specialize in ADHD. Many adult psychiatrists, although not all, are trained to treat the disorder.

Adult ADHD was not generally recognized by psychiatrists until the 1990s and psychiatry residencies took many years to design and train professors to teach adult ADHD care to residents. Current psychiatric residency graduates have received extensive training in ADHD care, while the majority of previous graduates learned about it through professional accreditation and continuing education programs.

Although this cannot be expected, most psychiatrists handle a considerable proportion of ADHD patients. When ADHD is co-occurring with depression, severe anxiety, bipolar illness, violent disorders, or other psychiatric diseases, psychiatrists are typically the best doctors to consult. Don't assume that all mental health professionals or primary care doctors are knowledgeable in treating ADHD. Some adult psychiatrists complete residencies without any training in ADHD, whereas other family physicians and internists have a specific interest in ADHD diagnosis and treatment.

A rising number of medical offices specialize in ADHD, and if you can locate one in your area, they are typically an excellent choice. When everyone in a clinic is focused on ADHD, office staff may provide valuable guidance and assistance.

When it comes to treating ADHD in adults, it appears that a mix of medication, skill training, and therapy is the most successful method. Adults with ADHD who have a treatment plan that includes medication and cognitive behavioral therapy may be able to control their symptoms better than those who solely take medication, according to research. Organizational abilities and self-esteem appear to be strengthened as well through this approach.

Importance of Seeking Professional Help

Untreated ADHD can disrupt daily living and make it more difficult to achieve your goals. It can have an impact on your job, and relationships. ADHD is treatable, and consulting with an ADHD specialist is a smart place to start.

Women with ADHD who do not seek treatment frequently have negative effects such as low self-esteem, drug abuse disorders, and suicide ideation. According to recent studies, women with ADHD had considerably lower lifespans than women without ADHD.

This condition is manageable for women with adequate support networks in place. If you have ADHD, there are several resources available to you. It can be a complicated disorder that can feel overwhelming to people who suffer from it. ADHD symptoms are curable with the correct treatment strategy.

An ADHD specialist can assist you in determining the most effective treatment option. This disorder is a lifelong condition, but a trained professional can help you reduce the severity of the symptoms you are experiencing. You can begin by speaking with your primary care doctor, who can get you started with a referral. It is critical to discover the correct ADHD expert for you, so you may need to diversify your search. You may look into a variety of options, including networking with individuals with the same issue. Word of mouth and personal referrals may be valuable information sources at times.

Whatever approach you take to find the right treatment for your disorder, it is important to seek professional help and not let it take over your life.

To maximize symptom management, most attempt a range of treatment strategies. It is typically better to start by trying one thing at a time to evaluate how the therapy affects you. Keep a journal when you introduce something new so you can track the progress of your efforts and understand the consequences of each method you try.

Be patient and consult your providers as needed. If changes are not happening as quickly as you would want them to, do not abandon treatment. It takes time for things to change. Before you give up on the treatment, look for methods to improve it.

ADHD experts are sadly scarce in comparison to the number of patients with ADHD who require treatment. The best option is not the one with the most attractive office or the friendliest doctor. It is the person in charge of symptom alleviation and effective life progression for the individual with ADHD. The outcome will develop over time, but thorough research today increases your chances of success.

Reach Out a Helping Hand

Dear reader,

I hope that you enjoyed reading my book.

As you embrace your diagnosis and implement strategies to help you live in a neurotypical world, you'll probably wish you'd known all of this sooner. You can't go back in time, but you can help someone else discover what you have.

Simply by sharing your honest opinion of this book on Amazon, you'll show other women with ADHD where they can find the information and strategies they've been searching for their whole lives.

As a self-published author, feedback can make a significant impact on the success of my book, so I would be very grateful if you could write a review on Amazon in your free time, I will read it personally.

Click here to leave your review on Amazon.

Your feedback, whether positive or negative, is greatly appreciated, and I value it all.

Thank you for your time and I look forward to reading your review.

Sincerely,

Tracy.

Scan to leave a review !

CONCLUSION

ADHD may make it challenging to handle the obstacles of daily life if not treated. The condition may involve mood swings, unhappiness, low self-esteem, eating disorders, risk-taking, and arguments with others. Yet many people with ADHD live happy, successful lives, and this workbook was the tool you needed all this time. Therapy makes dealing with life challenges easier. Monitoring your symptoms and routine doctor visits are essential. Sometimes treatments and medications that were beneficial in the past stop working for you. Your approach to treating ADHD may need to change. One thing is for sure, however, whether you choose, medication and therapy, or therapy and the heaps of tips given in this workbook, you can take over your ADHD and the life challenges it brings with it.

You have lived your life thinking you were different from your schoolmates, and girlfriends. It took years for you to get a proper and thorough diagnosis; one that was long overdue and very needed. This diagnosis has helped you understand and find yourself.

As promised, this workbook has covered a multitude of topics; from starting the day right to maintaining focus in a non-ADHD-friendly work environment. You will close this book having acquired tons of tips that you can utilize in your everyday life, and new activities which you can start scheduling in your days to help you manage your ADHD better. You will no longer struggle to manage your time or to make an important decision.

Keep this workbook in mind and come back to it if you start noticing that your relationships are plummeting because of your ADHD, whether romantic, familial, or corporate relationships. You have the tools to improve all of these. This workbook is not a one-time read, that you tick off your reading bucket list, but rather a reference you can always come back to whenever you need. Use the exercises and employ the activities suggested here because they are going to change your life. Make multiple copies of the exercises you find most helpful and use them as needed.

Here is what to take away from this workbook:

- Learn how to put yourself first and stop people-pleasing while jeopardizing your mental and physical health.
- Avoid burnout and learn how to find balance in your life.
- Practice self-compassion and treat yourself the same way you would a close friend.
- Follow the advice you would give to others.
- Seek help from professionals and use the tips given here to choose the best team to help manage your ADHD.
- Build links with other women with ADHD, through online communities and encourage each other.
- Find support groups in your local community and share the tips you have with others, and learn from them too.
- Make gratitude journaling part of your routine to minimize your negative thinking.
- Choose healthy eating habits over unhealthy comfort food.
- Join a gym and make physical activity a priority. If this is not for you, you can still listen to your favorite podcast as you take a walk around the area, or at a nearby park.
- Learn how to set boundaries and use the word "NO" a little more often than you usually do. You will not be acting selfish if you do that, but rather prioritizing yourself.

Apart from the tips and strategies in this workbook, there is one other takeaway you should take with you as you flip the last page. You matter and there has always been a perfectly good explanation for the way you felt and acted in your life to date. It is a pity that you did not have the diagnosis and explanation you deserved before today. You are ready to conquer the world now, fully armored with the life skills you need. Your life will no longer be impeded by your condition. You are more than your ADHD. You will bring value, happiness, strength, and positivity.

ABOUT THE AUTHOR

Tracy Neel, a dedicated advocate and an insightful mentor, is the author of the ADHD Workbook for Women; an essential guide tailored to empower and support women with ADHD in their day-to-day lives.

Having been diagnosed with ADHD as an adult, Tracy is well-acquainted with the unique challenges and complexities that women with ADHD face. After her diagnosis, she embarked on an intensive journey of self-discovery and learning, exploring various disciplines, including psychology, neuroscience, and behavioral therapy. As she gained valuable insights and implemented effective strategies to manage her ADHD, Tracy experienced a newfound sense of confidence, fulfillment, and personal growth.

Realizing the transformative potential of her newfound knowledge, Tracy decided to share her experiences and expertise with others, creating a resource specifically designed for women with ADHD. Her empathetic and compassionate approach to the subject, coupled with her first-hand understanding of the condition, has made her a sought-after mentor, coach, and advocate in the field.

Tracy has completed numerous courses and certifications in ADHD coaching and counseling, and she remains actively engaged in the latest research and developments related to ADHD. As a member of various professional organizations dedicated to supporting individuals with ADHD, Tracy works tirelessly to increase awareness and understanding of the condition, advocating for improved access to resources and support.

In addition to her work as an author and coach, Tracy is a passionate supporter of mental health initiatives and frequently volunteers her time to educate and raise awareness about ADHD in her community. She also facilitates workshops and support groups, creating a safe and nurturing environment for women with ADHD to share their experiences, learn from one another, and develop lifelong connections.

When she is not writing, coaching, or advocating for ADHD awareness, Tracy enjoys a variety of creative pursuits, such as painting, photography, and writing poetry. She is also an outdoor enthusiast who loves hiking, biking, and exploring nature with her beloved dog, Max. Tracy believes that cultivating a strong support network and engaging in activities that bring joy and relaxation are essential for living a fulfilling life with ADHD.

Made in the USA
Columbia, SC
22 June 2023